In the Presence of the Lord

Other Works by Al Hill

O Come, Let God Adore Us
And Other Sermons for Advent and Christmas

Not Exactly What They Expected
And Other Sermons for Holy Week and Easter

Our Evil—God's Good
And Other Sermons from Genesis through Joshua

Things That Kings Can't Do
And Other Sermons from Judges through 2nd Kings, and the Wisdom Books

Walking with Jesus
And Other Sermons from the Gospel of Matthew

God's Purpose for Your Faith
And Other Sermons from the Gospel of Mark, Hebrews, James and 1st Peter

From Jerusalem to Jericho
And Other Sermons from the Gospel of Luke and the Acts of the Apostles

Traits of the Shepherd
And Other Sermons from the Gospel of John, 1st John and Revelation

Making Peace with Your Father
And Other Sermons from Paul's Letters to the Romans and Corinthians

The Empty God
And Other Sermons from the Shorter Letters of Paul

DEAR TRINITY
Letters from a Pastor to His People

In the Presence of the Lord

*And Other Sermons
from the Psalms and the Prophets*

Al Hill

SOMMERTON
HOUSE

Cover design by the author.

The image of David, Isaiah and Jeremiah on the cover is a portion of a stained-glass window in St. Augustine's Anglican Church, in the Parish of Hamilton, in Brisbane, Australia. The image is from a photograph of the window taken by Laurence Shaw. It is used by the kind permission of the church and Mr. Shaw.

ISBN: 978-1-948773-11-9 (sc)

Library of Congress Control Number: 2018903980

To learn more about or purchase this or other works by Al Hill,
go to www.sommertonhouse.com,
or www.amazon.com/author/alhill.

Dedication

To the memory of my mother,
Margaret Stanfield Hill—

from whom I learned to sing (and love)
the great hymns of the Church,

and whose daily example of devotion to scripture
during my childhood
stimulated my life-long desire
to know the Bible better myself,
and to share its riches and power with others,
as she had shared them with me.

Contents

Dedication v

Preface ix

Sermons

From the Book of Psalms

Chapter 1. Sheep and Their Shepherd 7

Chapter 2. In a Not-So-Perfect World 13

Chapter 3. When You Give God Your Sin 23

Chapter 4. Happy Ending to a Sinful Story 31

Chapter 5. That the Next Generation Might Know 39

Chapter 6. For the Century Beyond 43

Chapter 7. Abiding in God's Abiding Word 51

Chapter 8. Restore Our Fortunes 59

From the Book of Isaiah

Chapter 9. On Earth as It Is in Heaven 69

Chapter 10. When the Leader is Gone 77

Chapter 11. In the Presence of the Lord 83

Chapter 12. The Everlasting God 89

Chapter 13. A Chosen Servant 97

Chapter 14. Lost and Found 105

From the Book of Jeremiah

Chapter 15. Since Before You Were Born 113

Chapter 16. One Way or the Other 123

From the Book of Lamentations

Chapter 17. Remembering This and That 131

From the Book of Ezekiel
Chapter 18. **When God Puts Your Life Back Together**..... 143

From the Book of Daniel
Chapter 19. **Put the Right Stuff In**............. 155
Chapter 20. **But If Not**.............. 165
Chapter 21. **Wise Ways in Wicked Days**............. 175

From the Book of Hosea
Chapter 22. **It's Who You Know**............. 185

From the Book of Amos
Chapter 23. **Religion, Inside and Out**............. 193

From the Book of Jonah
Chapter 24. **When You Think You're Going Under**........... 203

From the Book of Micah
Chapter 25. **Let's Take a Walk**............. 213

From the Book of Malachi
Chapter 26. **Refined Gifts and Givers**............. 225
Chapter 27. **Enough and More**............. 231

Indices

Sermon Texts in Biblical Order............. 238
Sermon Titles in Alphabetical Order............. 240
Related Sermons in Other Volumes............. 243
Sermon Texts in Lectionary Order............. 246
Additional Scriptures Referenced............. 250

Preface

One of the perks of being a pastor is that, if your church owns the building where it meets, you probably have your own key to it. You can come earlier or stay later than you have to—if you want to. Given how much time a pastor usually spends at church, such a desire might seem unlikely.

But from time to time, in various churches and chapels, I would linger after all others had left. I would sit on a pew in the empty sanctuary—or kneel, alone, at "the altar" (or before a communion table or prayer rail)—to "practice the presence of God."[1] In "being still," just for those few minutes, I "knew that God was God"[2]—and that I was mentally, morally, spiritually and physically in His presence. I was probably never more aware of the Lord's presence than in those sacred, solitary times.

The awareness of being in the presence of the Lord is not a common thing in our modern age of information and sensory overload. When you try to be aware of everything all the time—to be "connected"—it is unlikely that you will be aware of anything worthy of your undivided attention.

---

[1] Brother Lawrence (Nicholas Herman, 1605–1691), *The Practice of the Presence of God*, a Christian devotional classic.
[2] Psalm 46:10.

And yet, we are always in the presence of our Lord because He is always present with us—always waiting for us to turn our undivided attention to Him—always waiting to provide us a sense of the sacred in our lives so consumed by so much that is not.

But the problem itself is not new. It is an old, old problem. We know this is true because our Lord called prophets, centuries before He sent us Jesus Christ, to cry out to the undeserving people He had chosen to be aware of Him—and to live in unique relationship with Him. God gave His prophets words of judgment, on the one hand, and of hope, on the other. They condemned God's people when the people ignored God's presence—and comforted those same people when they sought Him.

When God's people did come into His presence, they sang the songs that He had given them for that purpose. King David and others were inspired to write songs of praise and thanksgiving for celebrating the Lord's goodness—and songs of petition and despair to give expression to their pain, sorrow, fear and need.

And thousands of years later, the words of the psalmists and the prophets still have the power to usher us into God's presence, whether the place we go is a "place alone," or one filled with others of like mind and spirit. I know this to be true, because I have used these words as the inspiration for my own devotions—and the basis for the sermons that follow in this book.

The good news is this: There is no one who cannot come into the presence of the Lord. It is what God would have you do.

৯৩

This book is part of a series that is 11 in number. This volume covers (generally) the last third of the Old Testament. However, some 15 sermons from these books of the Bible have not been included in this volume because they appeared previously in *O Come, Let Us Adore Him* and *Not Exactly What They Expected*, collections that deal with Advent and Christmas—and Holy Week and Easter—respectively. The final index of this book provides more detailed information about where to find those sermons.

On the other hand, the sermon "Restore Our Fortunes" (on page 57) also appears in *O Come, Let God Adore Us*, and "Enough and More" (on page 233) is also published in *God's Purpose for Your Faith*.

ॐ

As with previous volumes, the sermons you will find here were preached in Navy chapels and civilian churches over more than a decade. They were written to be heard, not read, and so the absence of vocal emphasis, facial expressions, body language and gestures will make understanding them more difficult in places.

However, you will have the advantage the original listeners did not have of re-reading a sentence or paragraph that may have confused you the first time around. You can flip back to previous pages to compare or clarify.

From time to time, the specific circumstances of the original congregation will become apparent. All sermons are preached within a context of shared experience and understanding. I trust you will be able to adapt what you read to your own life and perspective.

ॐ

The texts of the sermons have been printed before or within the body of the sermons for your convenience. The position of the scripture—and the specific version used—reflect the practice of the church or chapel in which the sermon was preached. In a number of cases, the original text was from an earlier edition of the New International Version (NIV), which is no longer available for publication. The English Standard Version (ESV) of the Bible has been substituted in those instances.

My practice is to capitalize nouns and pronouns that represent Father, Son or Holy Spirit, contrary to modern convention. In addition to expressing reverence, the practice also aids clarity. The exception to this practice is in the copyrighted texts of scripture, where pronouns referring to deity are printed as published.

৯৽৽৻

Several sermons are based on the same passage of scripture. That's because I usually followed the Revised Common Lectionary in the selection of texts and, over time, naturally returned to passages preached from previously. In my defense, I point out that few passages have all their meaning or power "mined" in just one effort by any preacher.

And, of course, the Old Testament readings were generally paired with Gospel or Epistle readings. Where the sermons addressed the second passage in a significant way, it, too, has been provided.

৯৽৽৻

To make the book more useful for my colleagues who are still preparing sermons—and for anyone who is reading for inspiration or enlightenment—several other indices have been provided. The footnote references throughout the book were not part of the original oral presentations, of course. But I hope they will be useful—and that the biblical references will help ground the assertions of the sermons solidly in scripture.

And, finally, I pray that you will find something in the sermons that follow that will lead you into the presence of the Lord. The hours spent in their preparation often did so for me.

৯৽৽৻

Sermons

From the Psalms

Psalm 23 KJV

[1] *The* LORD *is my shepherd; I shall not want.*
[2] *He maketh me to lie down in green pastures:*
  he leadeth me beside the still waters.
[3] *He restoreth my soul:*
  he leadeth me in the paths of righteousness for his name's sake.
[4] *Yea, though I walk through the valley of the shadow of death,*
  I will fear no evil: for thou art with me;
  thy rod and thy staff they comfort me.
[5] *Thou preparest a table before me in the presence of mine enemies:*
  thou anointest my head with oil; my cup runneth over.
[6] *Surely goodness and mercy shall follow me all the days of my life:*
  and I will dwell in the house of the LORD *for ever.*

৯৩

John 10:1-11 RSV

[Jesus said:]

¹ *"Truly, truly, I say to you, he who does not enter the sheepfold by the door but climbs in by another way, that man is a thief and a robber;* ² *but he who enters by the door is the shepherd of the sheep.* ³ *To him the gatekeeper opens; the sheep hear his voice, and he calls his own sheep by name and leads them out.* ⁴ *When he has brought out all his own, he goes before them, and the sheep follow him, for they know his voice.* ⁵ *A stranger they will not follow, but they will flee from him, for they do not know the voice of strangers."* ⁶ *This figure Jesus used with them, but they did not understand what he was saying to them.*

⁷ *So Jesus again said to them, "Truly, truly, I say to you, I am the door of the sheep.* ⁸ *All who came before me are thieves and robbers; but the sheep did not heed them.* ⁹ *I am the door; if any one enters by me, he will be saved, and will go in and out and find pasture.* ¹⁰ *The thief comes only to steal and kill and destroy; I came that they may have life, and have it abundantly.* ¹¹ *I am the good shepherd. The good shepherd lays down his life for the sheep."*

অ⳿৹

1.

Sheep and Their Shepherd

Psalm 23 KJV; John 10:1-11 RSV

The 23rd Psalm is the most famous psalm in the Bible, and almost certainly the most popular. It is also the most powerful, mending broken hearts at gravesides and sustaining failing hearts overwhelmed by crisis or awash in fear.

The psalm is compelling because it is simple:

"The LORD is my shepherd…"

That metaphor—that image—confronts you, and then the Psalmist unpacks it: *"The LORD is my shepherd* and because of that, I—lack—nothing! Every hunger—every thirst—is provided for. No dark moment is faced alone. No danger goes unchallenged."

"This is what I have experienced," says the Psalmist. "This is what I know."

And you know what? Across the centuries—across the globe—men and women who read it or hear it or memorize it don't say, "That's ridiculous!" They say, "That's right! Me, too! The Lord is my Shepherd. That's how I see things, too."

It's helpful—comforting—to have an image like a shepherd to look to when you're trying to imagine God. I'd much rather my God be a protecting, providing Presence than an angry, vengeful Judge or a cold and distant Mystery.

But to say that God is your Shepherd is also to say at the same time—or at least to imply—the other part of the equation: I am His sheep. It seems like an obvious next step in our understanding of things, but not all obvious steps get taken. Too many people don't make the sheep-and-shepherd, me-and-God, connection. They choose other animal analogies to embody their self-perception. Let me illustrate:

Some of you have cats as pets, and some of you have dogs. We all know they're very different animals. They seem to have very different perspectives. Someone has said that the difference is that a dog thinks: "This person feeds me and keeps me warm and comfortable. This person showers me with affection and attends to all my wants. This person must be a *god.*"

On the other hand, the cat thinks: "This person feeds me and keeps me warm and comfortable. This person showers me with affection and attends to all my wants. *I* must be a god."

In your relationship with God, it's important to know who's who. Who's the god and who's the "pet"? Who's the sheep and Who's the Shepherd?

The Psalmist says, "God takes me where I can eat and drink my fill. God provides me with moral guidance and spiritual renewal. God protects me from evil so effectively that even when I see it everywhere, I'm not afraid. He heals my wounds and makes me confident that what is to come in life will be even better than what I have experienced so far."

"The best way I know to describe what I have experienced," says the Psalmist, "is that this Provider and Protector is a God Who behaves toward me like a shepherd. What I experience is what sheep experience when a shepherd provides and protects them. Simply put: 'The Lord is my Shepherd; I am His sheep.'"

So far, so good. If you know that much, you know something important.

ॐ∽ॐ

But compared to what else there is to know, it really isn't much. Knowing something about God is good: God is like a shepherd to me. But imagine how much more there is to know!

A small-town newspaper carried a human-interest story about a 94-year old woman in a local nursing home and her daughter who came every day to be with her. The daughter, herself a senior citizen, lovingly combed her mother's hair and washed her face. She rolled her mother's wheelchair to the lunch room where she helped the elderly woman eat her food. This daughter hugged her mother and kissed her every day as she had done for so many, many years, and yet the mother's mind was so dim and her understanding so limited that she could only describe this one who loved her and provided for her most basic needs as "that lady who feeds me." That's all she knew.

But there was so much more.

What do sheep know about their relationship with their shepherd? Not much, really.

I am God's sheep. God is my Shepherd. God leads me, feeds me, protects me, provides for me and promises me a life rich in goodness and mercy. That's enough to justify the "shepherd" metaphor.

But Who is this shepherd God? Who is this mysterious Presence, this great and benevolent Power? Who is this God?

For the answer to that question, we have to look beyond the 23rd Psalm. Psalm 23 provides us the human perspective on a person's relationship with God.

Inspired?

Certainly.

Powerful?

Without a doubt.

But there is a difference between the human perspective and the divine perspective. For the divine perspective, we have to go to the New Testament—to the Gospel of John.

❧

In John, Chapter 4, Jesus said to a woman He met at a well, *"If you knew…who it is that is saying to you, 'Give me a drink,' you would have asked him and he would have given you living water."*[3]

Do you see the connection?

> *"The Lord is my shepherd…*
> *He leads me beside the still waters."*

In the tenth chapter of the Gospel of John, Jesus lays it out plainly. *"I am the good shepherd,"* He says. The Lord Who is our Shepherd is revealed to be not a mysterious, unknown deity, but a God Who became flesh and dwelled among us.[4]

We, like sheep, could not know the God Who is our divine Shepherd if we only had our human senses and intuition to go by. But our Shepherd God could cause us to know what He wants us to know.

It's called "revelation."

John said, *"No one has ever seen God, but the only Son…has made him known."*[5]

"The LORD is my shepherd," said the Psalmist.

"I am the good shepherd," said Jesus.

What a glorious discovery! What a glorious revelation!

৵৹

Do you remember the movie, *You've Got Mail?*[6] A young woman was communicating by email with someone who was always kind and compassionate. She savored every message she got from him because he somehow understood her in a way no one else did, and he seemed to know exactly what she needed to hear. She just didn't know who he was. He was a stranger: no name— no face.

---

[3] John 4:10, RSV.
[4] John 1:14.
[5] John 1:18, RSV.
[6] Movie *You've Got Mail!* 1998.

At the same time, she was confronted by someone who seemed to be an enemy. This man upended her world and made it impossible for her to live as she had before.

Gradually, however, she began to realize that this frustrating man with the familiar face and the famous name was not an enemy. She came to appreciate other things about him—good qualities. And yet, all the time, she yearned to know the identity of the other, unknown one who had been speaking so sweetly to her heart from the beginning.

And then one day, the person she had come to love more than anybody else revealed that he was also the mysterious stranger who had loved her all along.

Do you remember what she told him? "I wanted it to be you!"

And while you are depending on the Lord Who is your Shepherd—Whoever He is—He announces to you that He is Jesus Christ.

"I am the good shepherd," He says, "I made sure you lacked nothing. I made you lie down in green pastures. I led you beside still waters. I restored your soul. I led you in righteous paths even through dark valleys. Through all the hardships and difficulties—through all the uncertainties and sorrows—I protected you and provided for you and restored you. I am the Good Shepherd and I have proved it by laying down My life for you."

And can you say, "Oh, Jesus, I wanted it to be You!"? Isn't This Who you wanted your God to be? You can't be your own God. In this, if nothing else, cats are mistaken. A god has to be able to protect you and provide for you. Can you restore your own soul in a world like ours—in a life like yours?

You can tell Jesus, the Good Shepherd: "I want it to be You. I want the divine Shepherd Who has blessed me in so many ways all the days of my life to be the Savior Who gave His life, in love, for me. The Lord Jesus Christ is my Shepherd. His sheep am I."

Coming to this realization—accepting this revelation—is essential. Everyone is a sheep in comparison to God.

But, according to Jesus the Good Shepherd, not every sheep is His. Jesus says in John 10 that, in order to be His sheep, you have to hear His voice, know His voice, and follow Him.

He will go after stray sheep, of course. Even if you were the only one, He would leave the rest and come find you and bring you back to the safety of the fold.[7]

But

> *"All we like sheep have gone astray,"*

says Isaiah,

> *"we have turned every one to his own way."*[8]

So you're not the only one the Good Shepherd has had to rescue.

But remember, the Good Shepherd herds sheep, not cats. Do not think you are blessed because you deserve it.

Jesus calls His own sheep by name and leads them out, into this world and through it to the house of His Father. Do you hear His voice? Is the Lord Jesus Christ, the Good Shepherd, your Shepherd?

In the end, we're all sheep, really. Whose sheep are you?

(Ba)a-men.

❧

---

[7] Luke 15:3-7.
[8] Isaiah 53:6, RSV.

2.

In a Not-So-Perfect World

Psalm 32:1-5 RSV

¹ Blessed is he whose transgression is forgiven,
whose sin is covered.
² Blessed is the man to whom the LORD imputes no iniquity
and in whose spirit there is no deceit.
³ When I declared not my sin,
my body wasted away through my groaning all day long.
⁴ For day and night your hand was heavy upon me;
my strength was dried up as by the heat of summer.
⁵ I acknowledged my sin to thee,
and I did not hide my iniquity;
I said, "I will confess my transgressions to the LORD,"
and thou didst forgive the guilt of my sin.

❧

If this were a perfect world, winters would be short and mild, and rain would never fall on weekends—or days when you have errands to run. Parking places would always be available in front of your favorite stores, and cars would move out of your way on the interstate. If this were a perfect world, everybody would get along perfectly. There would be no mean or greedy or thoughtless people, and forgiveness would be totally unnecessary.

But this is not a perfect world. And so, you bundle up and carry an umbrella. You hike through parking lots and creep—inch by inch—through traffic jams. And people don't get along perfectly. In fact, things are happening all the time, it seems, that need forgiving.

In this less-than-perfect world, forgiveness is a necessity. In this less-than-perfect world, you and I are less than perfect. *We* are mean and greedy and thoughtless—some more thoroughly or more often than others, for sure—but all of us enough that we must be forgiven.

What does it mean to be forgiven? What does forgiveness accomplish?

❧

God's forgiveness is about saving us and saving our relationship with Him that sustains us. Sin attacks this relationship and God's forgiveness repairs it. Forgiveness, then, works to save our relationship with God—and our relationships with other people—from acts that would normally damage or even destroy them.

When a relationship is saved by forgiveness, it is saved by grace. After all, people who *need* to be forgiven do not *deserve* to be forgiven. You cannot demand it. You cannot buy it. You have no "right" to it. You forfeit any possible right to forgiveness by committing the very act that needs forgiving. To be forgiven is to receive a gift that is in no way deserved, and *that* is the very definition of "grace." The Psalmist experienced God's forgiving grace because God is a forgiving God.

But if you play your cards right, you can still prevent the forgiving God from forgiving you. Just refuse to confess your sin. Just pretend to God the way we pretend to each other: "I didn't do it." "It's not my fault." "You can't prove I did anything." "I don't know what you're talking about." "*You* don't know what you're talking about."

That approach won't get you very far with the person you've sinned against, and it won't get you anywhere at all with God. To come back into a relationship, you must come clean about your sin and your guilt. Otherwise, you are stuck with your guilt for the evil you did—as well as for the dishonesty with which you perpetuate that guilt. The guilt and dishonesty will become a permanent part of who you are, and over time, they will harden you inside and squeeze out the good that should have grown in their place. At first, the Psalmist hid and "protected" his sinfulness, and it festered within him—all because he refused to acknowledge the truth.

And there's more. If you do not confess your sin, someone else may be blamed for it and suffer unjustly in your place, which is more sin for you. If you do not confess your sin, you can still be blamed, but you can't be forgiven because you've twisted or hidden the truth. At the same time, resentment and distrust take charge and the anger people feel because you will not admit the sin eventually dwarfs the anger generated by the sin itself.

If you will not repent, you cannot receive forgiveness. The relationship remains broken. On the other hand, repentance and confession enable you to receive the forgiveness someone is giving. And forgiveness can save a marriage or a friendship, a professional association or the simple interaction with a stranger—one human being's relationship to another—which is the basis of a civil society. So it is to your benefit to be forgiven.

৵৹

But it is also to your benefit to forgive.

There is a story told about two lifelong enemies. They may have been brothers; I don't remember. One prayed for a blessing and God told him he could have anything he wanted, but his enemy would get the same thing twice over. The man thought for a moment, and then told God, "Make me blind in one eye."

15

In the real world, when you withhold your forgiveness, the math is reversed: you do twice as much damage to yourself as you do to the one you seek to hurt by your refusal to forgive. What happens when you do not forgive? God does not forgive you—and your moral superiority over the person who has sinned against you is immediately neutralized.

And Jesus teaches His disciples to pray, *"Forgive us our trespasses as we forgive those who trespass against us."*[9] Your forgiveness from God is linked to your forgiving of others—directly linked. Jesus says: *"…if you forgive men their trespasses, your heavenly Father also will forgive you; but if you do not forgive men their trespasses, neither will your Father forgive your trespasses."*[10]

"But how can I forgive him after what he's done?"

How could God forgive *you* after what *you've* done? Is the pain you have suffered—perhaps are still suffering—any greater than the pain God in Christ suffered for you—to forgive you?[11]

"How can I forgive her after what she's done?"

How can you not? Is the pain you are suffering now as great as the pain you will suffer if, by refusing to forgive, you prevent God from forgiving you?

Oh, the Bible does talk about an "unpardonable sin." Jesus says this unpardonable sin is *"blasphemy against the Holy Spirit."*[12] Many people apparently interpret this phrase to mean "doing something really bad *to me*" because they treat this "really bad something" as an unpardonable sin.

"You should forgive that person for what he did to you."

"I can't forgive him!"

And then there follows a description of the sin that is somehow "unpardonable."

---

[9] Matthew 6:12, also from *The Episcopal Book of Common Prayer*, 1928.
[10] Matthew 6:14-15, RSV.
[11] Romans 5:8.
[12] Luke 12:10.

"You can't forgive it?!" Since when is "blasphemy against the Holy Spirit" a sin against you personally, and how is a sin *against you,* "blasphemy against the Holy Spirit"?

It is true that some people just won't let you forgive them. They will not confess, repent or acknowledge their sin. But even here, you can still do the work of forgiveness. You can still decide to do the forgiving. You can position yourself to forgive, mentally, morally and emotionally, so that when that person does seek it and is ready to receive it, your forgiveness is there. And all the while, you will experience the benefits of forgiving, even if the other person refuses to benefit from being forgiven by you.

&

The truth is that you *can* forgive. If you will not forgive selflessly, then forgive selfishly. Do it for yourself. When you forgive, you align yourself with God. When you refuse to forgive, you line up against God, because God forgives and tells us to do the same.

We need to do a lot more forgiving than we do. The results of our refusal to forgive pile up in our lives like garbage in a summer sanitation strike. But in forgiving, you release the anger, hatred, and bitterness that will otherwise grow and fester around your pain. Then, your life will not be consumed by them, but will find room for love and joy and hope to take their place. You forgive so that *you* may live again.

Oh, the forgiver pays a price—always. Real forgiveness is not a simple statement of reassurance; it is a solemn declaration of a costly commitment. And once declared, forgiveness may take a good long time to complete. "I forgive you" may be better expressed by saying, "I have decided to undertake the process of forgiving you," for it is more a process than an event.

To forgive is to decide that the relationship at risk is more important than your natural desire to avoid the pain the transgression—and the transgressor—have caused you in the

17

relationship. Forgiveness begins in the mind, not in the heart. It begins in what you know, not in how you feel. If you wait until you *feel* like forgiving, you will never forgive.

Don't misunderstand me. To forgive is not to condone or overlook sin. God doesn't say a relationship is right or righteous when it isn't. But by forgiving, God makes a relationship right that wasn't. That is how God makes our relationship with Him what it ought to be. By forgiving, we restore our human relationships to what they can and should be as well.

The point of forgiveness is not to "let somebody off the hook." Forgiveness does not eliminate the need for accountability. Even forgiven, the person responsible may still have to undergo a proper punishment for the transgression. Nor does undergoing punishment guarantee or require that forgiveness will be given. The point of forgiveness is to restore the relationship, with or without the imposition of punishment.

The requirement to forgive does not require you to suspend reason and prudence. It does not require you to place yourself at the mercy of one you know is still intent on doing you harm. But you may still forgive—in fact, you must forgive—what someone did to you in the past, even if you cannot reasonably allow that person the opportunity to commit that sin—or others—against you in the future. You must forgive so that you do not continue to be the victim of the past sin.

And you can forgive. Jesus told Peter (and us), "Don't ever stop forgiving."[13] God never commands us to do what we cannot do. On the other hand, God frequently demands that we do things that we cannot possibly do by ourselves. God frequently demands that we do things we can only do with the help of the Holy Spirit. Jesus said, *"With men this is impossible, but for God, all things are*

---

[13] Matthew 18:22.

18

possible.[14] Even forgiving. We know this is true because God has forgiven us.[15]

So let's look at God's forgiveness. It's the model we must use for our own. How does God forgive?

The Psalmist, having experienced God's forgiveness firsthand in a dramatic way, analyzed it in detail and celebrated each step in the process. Listen to it again:

> *"Blessed is he*
> *whose transgression is forgiven,*
> *whose sin is covered.*
> *Blessed is the man*
> *to whom the LORD imputes no iniquity*
> *and in whose spirit there is no deceit."*

❧

God begins by forgiving the transgression. The term for "transgression" in Psalm 32 means willful disobedience, rebellion against authority. The violation puts the transgressor at the moral mercy of the One Who has been offended. Several responses are possible and, of these options, the injured party (in this case, God), chooses forgiveness. He does not have to, but He does.

It is a course of action that He has chosen, more than a single or simple act. God says, "I am terribly upset by what you have done. But I will not abandon our relationship because of it, even though you have given Me reason to." That's what you are saying when you choose to forgive, and you back it up with your behavior every day.

❧

That chosen course leads to a next step. When God forgives, He covers the sin. Sin is an ugly thing, once committed. It's a

---

[14] Matthew 19:26, RSV.
[15] Ephesians 1:7.

stinking mess. Sin brings shame and guilt to the sinner. But God does not rub the sinner's nose in it. Rather, He makes it a past event, over and done with. The Psalmist cried in anguish elsewhere, *"…my sin is ever before me!"*[16] But it won't be that way when he is forgiven. God won't bring it up. God won't point it out at every opportunity. And if you are to forgive like God, neither will you.

When you forgive, you don't go back to "the scene of the crime." You don't "build a shrine" to the pain inflicted on you. You bury the sin deep in an unmarked "grave" and then you avoid that particular "cemetery."

Forgive and forget? Can't be done; we're not built that way.

But you can decide not to devote your time and energy to remembering every painful detail. You can forgive and cover the sin.

❧❦

God forgives the transgression, covers the sin—and imputes no iniquity. God sees the need you have for forgiveness and decides to give it. Then He cleans up the mess your sin has caused. Then He defines you—sees you—not as the doer of dirty deeds that you are, but as one who is capable of good deeds. God treats you as you *could* be, not as you have been. He does not brand you with a permanent mark of your crime, but offers you a clean slate. And when you forgive, you must give the person a chance to be someone other than—someone more than—the evil person who sinned against you.

❧❦

The result of God's forgiveness is a change in the spirit, the very nature, of the sinner. The person who repents and receives God's forgiveness will be a changed person, inside. The evil inside

---

[16] Psalm 51:3, RSV.

that motivated the evil outside is removed and replaced by something different, something driven by gratitude for the saving grace of God's forgiveness. The goal of your forgiveness, and the sign of its success, is a similar change in the person you forgive, and the restoration of the relationship you share with him or her.

This is not a perfect world. Forgiveness is necessary here. You need to be forgiven, and you can be, if you repent. You also need to be forgiving, and you can be that, too, if you will. Forgive, in this not-so-perfect world, 'cause the perfect world is coming—for forgiven, forgiving people.

છ∙ৡ

Psalm 32:1-5 RSV

[1] *Blessed is he whose transgression is forgiven,*
whose sin is covered.
[2] *Blessed is the man to whom the* LORD *imputes no iniquity*
and in whose spirit there is no deceit.
[3] *When I declared not my sin,*
my body wasted away through my groaning all day long.
[4] *For day and night your hand was heavy upon me;*
my strength was dried up as by the heat of summer.
[5] *I acknowledged my sin to thee,*
and I did not hide my iniquity;
I said, "I will confess my transgressions to the LORD*";*
and thou didst forgive the guilt of my sin.

৯০৫

Luke 19:1-10 RSV

[1] *[Jesus] entered Jericho and was passing through.* [2] *And there was a man named Zacchae'us; he was a chief tax collector, and rich.* [3] *And he sought to see who Jesus was, but could not, on account of the crowd, because he was small of stature.* [4] *So he ran on ahead and climbed up into a sycamore tree to see him, for he was to pass that way.* [5] *And when Jesus came to the place, he looked up and said to him, "Zacchae'us, make haste and come down; for I must stay at your house today."* [6] *So he made haste and came down, and received him joyfully.* [7] *And when they saw it they all murmured, "He has gone in to be the guest of a man who is a sinner."* [8] *And Zacchae'us stood and said to the Lord, "Behold, Lord, the half of my goods I give to the poor; and if I have defrauded any one of anything, I restore it fourfold."* [9] *And Jesus said to him, "Today salvation has come to this house, since he also is a son of Abraham.* [10] *For the Son of man came to seek and to save the lost."*

৯০৫

3.

When You Give God Your Sin

Psalm 32:1-5; Luke 19:1-10 RSV

When I became a Navy Chaplain, I learned that Christians from other denominations sing hymns we never sang in our Southern Baptist churches. One old hymn I learned soon after I was assigned to my first chapel was sung every Sunday in the same place in the service where we sing the Doxology.[17] The words to that new-to-me-old-hymn went like this,

> "We give Thee but Thine Own,
> whate'er the gift may be.
> All that we have is Thine alone—
> a gift, O Lord, from Thee."[18]

The words are lovely and profound, and—but for one significant exception—completely true. Everything we have *is* a gift from God—except one thing. Everything we give—or at least *can* give—to God, already belongs to God—except for one thing.

And that one thing is our sin.

---

[17] A four-line stanza of praise written by Anglican Bishop Thomas Ken about 1709. See James D. Smith III, "Where Did We Get the Doxology?" This article is found at http://www.christianitytoday.com/history/issues/issue-31/where-did-we-get-doxology.html.

[18] William Walsham How, "We Give Thee But Thine Own," 1858.

We—all of us—have sin—and the sinful nature that causes us—compels us—to sin. But God does not cause us to sin. God did not cause sin to exist. He did not create it. He did not give it to us—as a gift or a curse.

God gave us *"every good…and…perfect gift"*[19]—of which sin is not one. And though everything good we possess is actually "on loan" from God, sin is something else—something *not* good and certainly not perfect—something we possess in ourselves apart from God.

And yet, sin is the one un-godly thing in us God invites us to give to Him. Though sin of any kind is totally alien to His perfect holiness, God invites us to rid ourselves of the evil within us by giving it over to Him—in repentance and confession.

And the sin that we do give to God ceases to exist as soon as we give it, because it no longer resides in us, where it did and could exist. And it cannot reside in God as sin, because in Him there can be *no* sin at all.[20] When we give God our sin, it is destroyed as sin, and becomes merely another means for God's grace to work its mysterious wonders in our wicked, fallen world.

But how hard it is to give your sin to God! Like the demons Jesus cast out of one poor soul in the Bible, demons who begged to be sent into a herd of pigs rather than go before God as they were,[21] we don't want to come clean with God about our sin, or do anything with it that will upset the convenient contours of our lives too much.

So the options are basically two: confess or keep quiet.

ॐ⊶

The Psalmist tried the "Keep Quiet" approach first. When he could have confessed his sin, he didn't. And as a result, he began to rot away from the inside out. He was in misery from morning

---

[19] James 1:17, RSV.
[20] 1 John 1:5.
[21] Mark 5:1-17.

till night—because, from every morning to every night, God was against him—and not in a passive way. God's hand was heavy upon him, which is only natural, because God has a vested interest in "going after" sin, because that's what's messing up His wonderful Creation—and what keeps getting in the way of His divine repair work.

When it comes to the business of confession, "keeping quiet" means "keeping sin." And the Psalmist found that he just couldn't keep it up.

So he went the other way.

ॐॐ

The Psalmist came clean about his sin. He "owned" it before God: "Yes, Lord, that mess is mine"—which God knew all along, of course, but He couldn't do anything redemptive about it because the one responsible wouldn't take responsibility.

Redemption requires repentance. Without it, there can only be retribution—of the divine variety. So, no stone-walling—no cover up. Just stand up straight—or bow down humbly—and tell God the truth, so He can take your sin off your slate.

What does the Psalmist say happened?

"I acknowledged…I did not cover…I confessed to God…and God forgave."

Simple.

ॐॐ

But what does that mean, exactly? What actually happens when you give your sin to God the way the Psalmist did?

Well…some amazing things. They're listed right there at the beginning of the Psalm, like the last chapter in a novel that's been shifted to the beginning of the story, so you will know how it all ends up before you even start. And it's a very happy ending—or beginning!

"*Blessed* is he…happy…fortunate…lucky…."

"*Hurray* for you—if…your transgression is forgiven—your sin covered!"

"*Wow*…if God doesn't count any iniquity against you anymore!"

"If God has made it so that your sin is so completely gone from you that you don't even have to deceive yourself about it—and don't feel a need to try to deceive God about it anymore—*Hallelujah*!"

There are several things happening here. The first is that when you repent and confess—when you give your sin to God—your transgression—your rebellion against God's divine authority—is forgiven—pardoned—in full—forever. God declares a cease-fire in His attack on the sin in you, and therefore, on you. You are no longer a target of God's righteous wrath because of your sin.

That's a wonderful thing—worth celebrating all by itself—but it's not by itself. When you decide to stop trying to hide your sin from the God Who sees and knows everything,[22] the sin that you could not cover up, God does—but for your sake, not His. God covers the sin of the sinner who repents so that you do not have to wallow in the mire of your own making. God loves you too much to make you do that when you have confessed—though He would and has done exactly that, to push you to the point of the confession you need to make, to get past the problem and your separation from Him that your sin has produced.

When you give God your sin, as far as God is concerned, you don't have it anymore, and so God doesn't see you or treat you as though you do—or ever did. To God, you are what you have let Him make you—not what you made yourself when you were trying unsuccessfully to make yourself something else. God counts no iniquity against you. In His book—and that's a really important book—you're okay.

ঔৎকী

---

[22] Job 28:12, 23-24; 1 John 3:20.

All this is good stuff—stuff that you can understand God doing because of Who, and how wonderful, God is. But then the Psalmist goes on to say what may be the most amazing thing of all: When you give your sin to God in genuine repentance and confession, God makes *you* more wonderful, too. He changes who *you* are. He makes *you* more like Himself. Deception is dismissed from your spirit just like it is absent from His.

The Psalmist knows this from experience, apparently. And he's so happy about it that he's ready to "high-five" everybody in the house—God's holy House. "*Hurray* for whoever has figured out what I have! *Hallelujah* for a God Who will let me give Him my sin!"

Centuries later, somebody put what the Psalmist was saying this way: *"If we confess our sins, He is faithful and just to forgive us our sins and to cleanse us from all unrighteousness."*[23]

Or, to turn a phrase,

> "We give Thee but *our* own,
> whate'er the *sin* may be.
> *When all the sin* we have is Thine,
> *what* a gift, O Lord, from Thee!"

Can you give your sin to God?

Confess it and see.

❧

---

[23] 1 John 1:9, RSV.

Psalm 51:1-17 RSV

¹ *Have mercy on me, O God,*
  according to thy steadfast love;
according to thy abundant mercy
  blot out my transgressions.
² *Wash me thoroughly from my iniquity,*
  and cleanse me from my sin!
³ *For I know my transgressions,*
  and my sin is ever before me.

⁴ *Against thee, thee only, have I sinned,*
  and done that which is evil in thy sight,
so that thou art justified in thy sentence
  and blameless in thy judgment.

⁵ *Behold, I was brought forth in iniquity,*
  and in sin did my mother conceive me.
⁶ *Behold, thou desirest truth in the inward being;*
  therefore teach me wisdom in my secret heart.

⁷ *Purge me with hyssop, and I shall be clean;*
  wash me, and I shall be whiter than snow.
⁸ *Fill me with joy and gladness;*
  let the bones which thou hast broken rejoice.
⁹ *Hide thy face from my sins,*
  and blot out all my iniquities.

¹⁰ *Create in me a clean heart, O God,*
  and put a new and right spirit within me.
¹¹ *Cast me not away from thy presence,*
  and take not thy holy Spirit from me.

¹² *Restore to me the joy of thy salvation,*
and uphold me with a willing spirit.
¹³ *Then I will teach transgressors thy ways,*
and sinners will return to thee.

¹⁴ *Deliver me from bloodguiltiness, O God,*
thou God of my salvation,
and my tongue will sing aloud of thy deliverance.
¹⁵ *O Lord, open thou my lips,*
and my mouth shall show forth thy praise.
¹⁶ *For thou hast no delight in sacrifice;*
were I to give a burnt offering,
thou wouldst not be pleased.
¹⁷ *The sacrifice acceptable to God*
is a broken spirit;
a broken and contrite heart, O God,
thou wilt not despise.

৯•৭

4.

Happy Ending to a Sinful Story

Psalm 51:1-17 RSV

Sometimes, when you read the Bible, it doesn't make much sense: strange names, stranger customs—ancient history from a faraway place. On the other hand, sometimes when you read the Bible, you know exactly what it's talking about. You turn a page and there it is: the simple, undeniable truth—the truth about your life, your heart, your need. Today is one of those times. Today the Bible paints our picture. It tells our story. It's called "Psalm 51."

The first thing we see in this biblical "mirror" is that we are sinners.

But is this a true reflection? Are we sinners? I hear a lot of people these days saying things like, "I'm a good person," and "I deserve to be happy."

Are they right? Was one of those popular TV preachers onto something when he suggested a while back that what we call "sin" is really just "a negative self-image"? Certainly no one wants to be saddled with a negative self-image. And there can't be anything wrong with wanting to be happy. The Bible even says that when God created humanity, He called the result "very good."

So which is it, "good person" or "sinner"?

31

The answer is that you and I are sinners. No amount of sophisticated rationalizing or clever camouflaging will change that fact. We are sinners. To say otherwise is either a dangerous self-deception or a flat-out lie. 1 John says, *"If we say we have no sin, we deceive ourselves and the truth is not in us."*[24]

"All we like sheep have gone astray,"[25] says Isaiah.

"All have sinned and come short of the glory of God,"[26] says Paul, and, *"There is none righteous, no, not one."*[27]

It's not a pretty picture, but it is an accurate one.

Here in Psalm 51 is a sinner who knows he's a sinner:

> *"I know my transgressions,*
> *my sin is always before me...."*

"I've always been a sinner." Is this just one of those negative self-images? No, this is an example of the kind of painful honesty that is the first step in the most important transition a human being can make. That person who asserts her own goodness, or claims a "right" to happiness, is usually trying to justify more sinful behavior.

But the person who comes clean with himself about his real spiritual and moral condition is then—and only then—in a position to be made, or re-made, "good," and to receive genuine happiness, not as a right, but as an unmerited gift. I am a sinner, and I know it. What about you?

⊱⊰

So, okay, we're sinners. What's the big deal? Isn't everybody? Yes, everybody is a sinner. But don't let that commonality lull you into a fatal indifference. Sin is the spiritual version of some deadly disease spreading rapidly throughout the land. Wouldn't you want to get vaccinated against it? Or more accurately, if you were actually

---

[24] 1 John 1:8, RSV.
[25] Isaiah 53:6, RSV.
[26] Romans 3:23, RSV.
[27] Romans 3:10, RSV.

already dying from it, wouldn't you rush to take the medicine that could save your life? Sin is a killer. It eats at your spirit and destroys your life-sustaining relationship with God. But if you are to be successfully treated, you must first acknowledge that you have the infection.

And sin is an ugly infection.

"Blot out my transgressions,"

he prays.

> *"Wash away my iniquity*
> *and cleanse me from my sin....*
> *Cleanse me...*
> *wash me....*
> *Hide your face from my sins*
> *and blot out all my iniquity."*

Here is someone who sees his sin clearly. I visited with a woman who had been diagnosed with cancer and scheduled for surgery to remove the tumor. I asked if she was nervous about being operated on. She surprised me by saying, "I just want them to get this thing *out* of me."

If you know you're a sinner, and you understand the damage sin can do in your life, more than anything else, you'll just want someone to get it out of you.

But here's where things get a little tricky.

❧

It turns out that the only One who can fix our sin problem is the One against whom the evil of our sin is ultimately directed. Let me shift from a medical to a legal model: Our sin is a crime against the Judge Himself. Can you imagine what that is like?

A fellow from my hometown in Alabama ended up in prison in Kentucky, near where I was going to seminary many years ago. His father knew my father and asked if I would visit him. And several times, I did.

The young man told me he had been caught in the act of robbing a jeweler in a little mining town up in the mountains. He came to understand the full extent of his troubles later when he learned that the man he robbed at gunpoint was his judge's Sunday School teacher.

When he stood before the judge, it wasn't just about breaking the law; the judge was personally offended.

The Psalmist confesses,

"Against you, and you only, have I sinned...."

That's not literally the case, of course, for him or any of us. But Jesus said,

"What you do to the least of these...you do unto me."[28]

This is true whether it is "ministry to" or "sin against." Just as we talk about "crimes against the state," so we also recognize that all sins are committed ultimately against God. And God is the ultimate Judge of all. As I said, here it gets tricky.

Some people see the problem—our sin versus God's judgment—and despair. How many times have I heard people say, "I've done things in my life that I know God would never forgive"? They can only imagine themselves as "sinners in the hands of an angry God,"[29] and they give up all hope. They live a life shrouded in the dark shadows of guilt and foreboding, waiting for the divine punishment they are sure must one day come. "I am a sinner. God is a righteous Judge. I am doomed." And there their logic gets stuck.

☙❦

But look, there is more. *Hallelujah*, there's so much more! Here is a genuine, bona fide sinner who gathers up the mess he's made of his life like something in one of those heavy-duty trash bags, and takes it, of all places, right to the Judge he has sinned against:

---

[28] Matthew 25:40, 45.
[29] Jonathan Edwards, "Sinners in the Hands of an Angry God," 1741.

"Have mercy on me, O God,
according to Your unfailing love;
according to Your great compassion...."

Yes, God is a righteous judge. But God is more. Our God is also merciful. Our God is compassionate. Our God loves us.

Yes, God hates sin. But the unfailing love of this holy God for His children—His poor, sinful children—is greater even than His hatred for sin.

How do we know this? Is the revelation of scripture not evidence enough? Is the life of Jesus and His death on the Cross not the ultimate proof?

So, even though we're sinners, there's nothing to fear from our loving God, right?

Not quite. Our God is patient with sinners and so may postpone the punishment they deserve, to allow them time to repent.

But God is not permissive about sin. He does not condone it or accommodate Himself to it. As long as you embrace your sin, God will not embrace you. The Psalmist understood this and so prayed, *"Do not cast me from Your presence...."*

When I was stationed in Brunswick, Maine, there was a young lady in our chapel with a strong-willed and sometimes defiant little girl. As children will do, this one started pitching temper tantrums when she didn't get her way: kicking, screaming, "the whole nine yards." This conscientious mother tried reasoning and scolding, threats—and worse. Nothing phased this little girl when she got going.

And then one day, this loving parent said to her rebellious child, "I will not put up with this behavior any more. I'm going to my room and I'm locking the door. I won't come out as long as you keep acting like this." For a while, the little girl screamed at the locked door, but her mother would not come out—or let her in. It wasn't long before the tantrums stopped for good. The little girl

discovered she couldn't stand to be without her mother's loving presence. And the sinful Psalmist cried out to his heavenly Father,
"Take not Thy holy spirit from me!"
"No matter what I've done, don't make me live without You."
And, of course, we don't have to live without God.
"A broken and contrite heart, O God,
You will not despise,"
says the Psalmist.

Look at your own life experience. If someone you love comes to you with a broken and contrite heart, confessing his sin against you and pleading for your forgiveness, will you harden your heart and reject him? No, you will find a way to forgive, to make things right between you. And so God will do with you and me, for His mercy is deeper, His compassion is broader, and His love is far, far greater than any we could generate within ourselves.

These words we've used to describe God are interesting words. The word for "love" in the Bible refers to a "steadfast covenant loyalty," like what keeps a marriage going, through thick and thin, year after year, for a lifetime. The word for "mercy" refers to "one's deepest feelings for another." It's also used to describe how a mother feels toward her baby. And "compassion"? It means "to suffer with," as in, *"while we were yet sinners, Christ died for us."*[30]

So what do you do? You are a sinful person, and God is a merciful, compassionate, and loving God. Isaiah says,
"Seek the LORD while he may be found;
call upon him while he is near.
Let the wicked forsake his way
and the unrighteous man his thoughts.
Let him return to the LORD,
that he may have mercy on him,
and to our God,
for he will abundantly pardon."[31]

---

[30] Romans 5:8, RSV.
[31] Isaiah 55:6-7, RSV.

1 John puts it this way, *"If we confess our sins, he is faithful and just to forgive us our sins, and cleanse us from all unrighteousness."*[32]

"Cleanse me...and I will be clean; wash me and I will be white as snow." What does God do when He hears the sinner's cry, when He sees the contrite heart, when He accepts the sinner's confession, when He forgives the awful sin?

Well, sinners, the list of prizes is quite impressive. God starts by saving you from the judgment you deserve. Then God creates in you a pure heart. Then God renews a steadfast and obedient spirit in you. God teaches you the deepest kind of wisdom and restores a sense of joy in you about the whole saving experience. Each of these benefits of God's forgiveness deserves a sermon of its own, which, alas, must wait for a later day. But you should still be able to make out the overall picture.

Psalm 51 is the instruction guide for giving your sinner's story a happy ending.

What kind of happy ending?

Paul says, *"The wages of sin is death—but the gift of God is eternal life through Christ Jesus our Lord."*[33]

Wow! Eternal life! Sinners saved by grace! Can you *believe* it?

More importantly, *will* you...?

☙❧

---

[32] 1 John 1:9, RSV.
[33] Romans 6:23, RSV.

Psalm 78:1-7 RSV

[1] *O my people, hear my teaching;*
listen to the words of my mouth.
[2] *I will open my mouth in parables,*
I will utter hidden things, things from of old—
[3] *what we have heard and known,*
what our fathers have told us.
[4] *We will not hide them from their children;*
we will tell the next generation
 the praiseworthy deeds of the LORD,
his power, and the wonders he has done.
[5] *He decreed statutes for Jacob*
and established the law in Israel,
which he commanded our forefathers
to teach their children,
[6] *so the next generation would know them,*
even the children yet to be born,
and they in turn would tell their children.
[7] *Then they would put their trust in God*
and would not forget his deeds
but would keep his commands.

❧

5.

That the Next Generation Might Know

Psalm 78:1-7 RSV

"Give ear, O my people, to my teaching."

೧ಎം

The Psalmist has become a teacher in Psalm 78. His call is not to worship, but to learn. And what are God's people to learn? Things their parents and grandparents told them, passed down by ancestors who lived long before them. Things so old their origins are lost in time. Things that remain true across time itself. Things no one of God's people should ever be allowed to not know. And we will see why in a moment.

God's people are to learn things whose truth is so deep and mysterious and profound that they have to be conveyed in story if anyone is to be able to understand them. And so, the Psalmist says, "I will open my mouth in a parable, a story—the story of God and His relationship with people, the story of a particular people in relationship with a particular God—the story of a people who come, finally, to be your people—to be you. I will open my mouth and tell you your story."

And long after the Psalmist is dead and gone and all but forgotten, Another will come and take up the story and open His mouth in parables.[34] Another will utter the mysterious, timeless truths of God and what God is doing for His people. He will tell about ungrateful sons[35]—and uncaring leaders[36]—and bridesmaids who are not ready when the bridegroom suddenly arrives.[37] And every story will contain a revelation of divine, eternal truth. Every story will be about God—and you.

This One will tell The Story in stories, and He will tell it in deeds that will become the fulfillment of the ancient story. And just as generations before Him told the story, so will each generation after Him tell it. Including yours.

You are to hear the story of a people and their God and understand that they are your people, and this is your God. You are to learn, and you are to teach. You are to learn the deep and mysterious things of God—the glorious deeds and the mighty power and the wondrous miracles of this particular God. And you are to teach them to the coming generation—the children, not so much of your generation, but of the generations that have gone before you. "We will not hide [what] our ancestors have told us from *their* children," says the Psalmist. Not *our* children—*their* children. The next generation is *their* heritage even more than it is *ours.*

Look at the process God commanded His people to undertake: One generation of people (Let's call them "Generation A.") is to teach their children (Generation B) so that *their* children (Generation C), who are not even *born* as A is teaching B, will have even a possibility of knowing what Generation A has known—which is essential, for C is responsible to God to rise up and teach *their* children (Generation D) what A had taught B long before. Generation D, and every generation in the alphabet to follow, must

---

[34] Matthew 13:34.
[35] Luke 15:11-32.
[36] Luke 18:1-5.
[37] Matthew 25:1-12.

know the story of God's saving presence and power if they are to set their hope in God and keep His commandments.

For an individual to forget the works of God is bad—for that individual and for his family. For a generation to forget what God has done—and therefore to fail to teach the next generation—is disastrous, because every generation is dependent on the memory and the teaching of all the generations that have come before it.

Those who have been taught what God has done, throughout all generations, will know what God is doing now—and will do in the future. And they may respond, in faithfulness and love, to this God Who has proven His faithfulness and love to them from the very beginning.

Those who have not been taught will not know, and so will not respond as God desires. The generation that has not heard and does not know the mighty works of God among them becomes a stubborn and rebellious generation. And they suffer at the hands of a righteous God Who actually wanted to bless.

A generation that rejects the old wisdom—the divine wisdom of God revealed throughout human history—in favor of its own newly-minted certainties (as this generation has) will not be revered by the next one. The end result of such rejection is a poor and dangerous legacy that can only say, "Figure it out for yourselves. You're on your own. Good luck."

It is not enough that we worship God, even as faithfully and fervently as we do here. We must learn what countless generations of God's people have passed along to us: the deep and ancient stories that convey the message of God's love and purpose for us. And we must teach the next generation so that future generations will have even a chance of knowing what is necessary for *their* salvation. This is our calling. This is our vision. This must be our legacy.

ॐ

Psalm 78:1-7 RSV

¹ O my people, hear my teaching;
listen to the words of my mouth.
² I will open my mouth in parables,
I will utter hidden things, things from of old—
³ what we have heard and known,
what our fathers have told us.
⁴ We will not hide them from their children;
we will tell the next generation
the praiseworthy deeds of the LORD,
his power, and the wonders he has done.
⁵ He decreed statutes for Jacob
and established the law in Israel,
which he commanded our forefathers
to teach their children,
⁶ so the next generation would know them,
even the children yet to be born,
and they in turn would tell their children.
⁷ Then they would put their trust in God
and would not forget his deeds
but would keep his commands.

❧

6.

For the Century Beyond

Psalm 78:1-7 RSV

In less than 48 hours, the polls will open, in this state and others in the eastern part of our country. Thousands have already cast their votes where laws allow. Much is riding on the outcome of this Presidential election. I am deeply concerned about who will win and I would like to urge you all to go to polls on Tuesday and vote for the candidate of my choice.

I have resisted the desire to use this sermon to express my preference—or God's—between the two men running for President. Those who share my preference may be disappointed; those who do not, will surely be relieved. (See me after the service if you really must know.)

Electing a man President of the United States will ensure that he has a significant impact on the events of the four years of his term—for good or ill—and for some number of years beyond. The same is true, to some lesser degree, for those elected to any political office. People who are famous or wealthy or hold powerful positions in great organizations are expected to have a significant influence on people and events around them.

But what of the rest of us? What if you've never been elected to any office higher than chairman of the committee nobody wants

43

to be on? What if your wealth is limited to the monthly ebb and flow of your checkbook and, if you're lucky, a little left over for your old age? What if your fame doesn't extend to the end of your block? What impact can you ever hope to have in this world if you're nobody special—just an average guy or gal?

And do you care?

It may surprise you to know that just about everybody cares. This chapel is filled today with people who care about their impact on this world—who care very much about what their lives will have accomplished in the time allotted to them. And you are probably one of them.

Depending on your age and your sense of where you are on your life's journey, you may approach this subject by wondering what you will accomplish with the promise of a lifetime stretching out before you. You may be one who looks at the many activities and responsibilities in your life right now and wonder whether the work you are doing is worth the effort. Or, you may be well along in years and trying to measure the value of the life you have lived, or wondering if there is anything left for you to accomplish with it.

What I have to tell you today will be of greatest value to those of you at the beginning of the long march through life. Will it be wasted on those at the other end? I hope not, but you be the judge. You may also judge whether what I am telling you is true at all.

First, let me provide a bit of biblical context: In Psalm 8, the Psalmist asks God,

> *"[W]hat is man that thou art mindful of him,*
> *and the son of man that thou dost care for him?*
> *Yet thou hast made him little less than God,*
> *and dost crown him with glory and honor.*
> *Thou hast given him dominion*
> *over the works of thy hands;*
> *thou hast put all things under his feet...."*[38]

---

[38] Psalm 8:4-6, RSV.

In Genesis, God tells the human race He has just created, *"Be fruitful and multiply, ...fill the earth and subdue it and have dominion over"* everything else created.[39] Paul says, *"...we are ambassadors for Christ, God making His appeal through us."*[40] Christ Himself said, *"Follow me, and I will make you fishers of men."*[41]

What's the point? We are important to God and God has a purpose in creating us. This is true for all humanity, and it is true for each individual. Consider what this means for you personally: Your very existence is the result of a choice God made, and in choosing to cause you to exist, God has assigned a purpose for your life, a mission that your life is to fulfill.

Now before you give yourself a headache trying to figure out what that purpose could be, let me remind you that God has not left it a mystery. The purpose for your existence is the same as the purpose for my existence and the existence of every person who ever lived—save One.

Jesus Christ was born to die in just payment for our sins. That was *His* purpose. Everyone else exists to *participate* in God's redemption of His Creation through Christ's sacrifice on the Cross. Everyone else exists to be God's instrument pointing the world to Christ. So far, so good. Basic stuff. Christian Gospel 101.

But remember that God, our Creator, is an eternal God. That's why we and the Bible say, *"From everlasting to everlasting, thou art God."*[42] And God has been working this plan of redemption a long time—since the very first act of human disobedience broke the covenant of Creation and sin slid into the place where simple faith and fidelity were intended to be.[43]

And recently, by comparison, you and I came along. Now, we who are Christians will spend eternity with God in heaven. And in

---

[39] Genesis 1:28, RSV.
[40] 2 Corinthians 5:20, RSV.
[41] Matthew 4:19, RSV.
[42] Psalm 90:2, RSV.
[43] Genesis 3.

the eternal perspective of God, it won't be long before all of us get there. One day, your life on earth will be over.

But not your impact.

You see, your life is a gift that God gives to you. It is your most valuable physical possession. You can "spend" your life any number of ways. You can waste it. Or you can invest it. Like money, life is a valuable commodity that you can invest in view of a greater return.

There are some simple rules to investing, and they apply to financial investing and to spiritual investing alike. One is that the more you invest your capital and the earlier you invest it and the longer you leave it invested, the greater the return will be.

The impact of your life, if invested properly, outlives the "principal." In other words, if you are wondering what impact your life is having, you're wondering the wrong thing. If you're wondering what impact your life has had, you're wondering the wrong thing. The greatest impact of your life cannot be measured during your lifetime, or even at the end of it.

When Henry Kissinger was our Secretary of State, he asked the Chinese Premier Zhou Enlai what he thought the greatest impact of the French Revolution (of 1789) was on world history. The premier responded, "It is too early to tell."[44]

And it is too early to tell what the ultimate impact of your life will be because the ultimate impact of your life will not be experienced in your lifetime; it will be experienced in the century after you are dead and buried.

Exodus 34 tells the story of an encounter between God and Moses at Mount Sinai:

---

[44] In researching this anecdote further for this book, I learned that Zhou probably misunderstood the context of the question in translation, and thought Kissinger was asking about the more recent student protests of the late 1960s in France. Obviously, the original (mis)understanding is more interesting and invites greater thought and reflection.

*⁵ Then the LORD came down in the cloud and stood there with him and proclaimed his name, the LORD. ⁶ And he passed in front of Moses, proclaiming, "The LORD, the LORD, the compassionate and gracious God, slow to anger, abounding in love and faithfulness, ⁷ maintaining love to thousands, and forgiving wickedness, rebellion and sin. Yet he does not leave the guilty unpunished; he punishes the children and their children for the sin of the fathers to the third and fourth generation."*⁴⁵

ॐ∞ॐ

Well, if a compassionate and gracious God will punish the sin of a father through a third and fourth generation, surely He would *bless* the commitment of a righteous parent (or any person) for just as long or longer. If a generation is about 25 years (and they seem to be on average), then four of them could stretch over a hundred years—a century—after a person's death.

The point and purpose of your life is not this minute, or today, or this year, or even the rest of your life. God has caused you to "be" so that you may have a mighty impact for His kingdom, an impact that will be established and grow during your lifetime with such strength that it will continue to build like a tidal wave in others in the generations after you. Am I making this up? I don't think so.

Listen to the first seven verses of Psalm 78:

¹ O my people, hear my teaching;
listen to the words of my mouth.
² I will open my mouth in parables,
I will utter hidden things, things from of old—
³ what we have heard and known,
what our fathers have told us.
⁴ We will not hide them from their children;
we will tell the next generation
the praiseworthy deeds of the LORD,
his power, and the wonders he has done.

---

⁴⁵ Exodus 34:5-7, NIV.

⁵ He decreed statutes for Jacob
and established the law in Israel,
which he commanded our forefathers
to teach their children,
⁶ so the next generation would know them,
even the children yet to be born,
and they in turn would tell their children.
⁷ Then they would put their trust in God
and would not forget his deeds
but would keep his commands.

ঔৎ৶

The English poet John Donne wrote that
"No man is an island, entire unto himself.
Every man is a piece of the continent,
a part of the main."[46]

You do not have to be rich or famous or powerful by the world's measure to change the world. You will change it just by living. But if you see that the individual words and deeds of your life can form a vast investment in the lives of others, now—and especially in generations to come—how much greater is the appreciation you will have for your life's potential—how much more is your life worth now that you know you have the opportunity to invest it now for tremendous profit in the century beyond?

And how much clearer is the vision of how you are to live when you understand that the purpose for your having lived will be revealed fully only when your body has long since been laid in the grave?

"But I want to see what impact my life has had on the world!"

Don't worry; if you're a Christian, you'll see it just fine, even a century beyond your death.

---

[46] John Donne, Meditation 17, *Devotions upon Emergent Occasions*, 1624.

It is as though the things you say and do in life are like countless pebbles you cast into a pond, the pond of your family, your community, your circle of friends and acquaintances. The stone is cast and the water ripples. The deed is done, and the impact grows—the circle widens—with the passage of time. God's intention is that you ripple the pond for the century beyond—the century beyond your life on earth.

And how do you go about rippling the pond of life, especially if you're not rich or powerful or known and adored by countless fans in nameless mobs? The Psalmist says,

> *[T]ell the next generation*
> *the praiseworthy deeds of the LORD,*
> *his power, and the wonders he has done...*
> *so the next generation would know them,*
> *even the children yet to be born,*
> *and they in turn would tell their children."*

The secret to a mega-impact life is to introduce the next generation to God and tell them what God has done for them— for all of us. If you would be a world-changer, show your children and others, early on, that there is a "pond" to be rippled for God. Show them how to ripple the pond with their lives and how to teach the generations beyond them to do the same.

If you know that God has devised a system in which you are guaranteed to be a world changer, and that the impact of your life reaches its full effect only in the century after your death, what impact does that knowledge have on the way you live your life?

Well, for starters, you will be able to put the setbacks and disappointments of the moment in their proper perspective as inconveniences that do not long deter you or your pursuit of the ultimate goal. You will be able to make decisions each day based on ultimate significance rather than immediate impulse or selfish interest. And you will see yourself as an ever-developing asset to God, regardless of the meaning or value others may place on what they see of your life.

If you are young, when you understand your potential for ultimate impact, you will want to make sure you pick a marriage partner who will help you make the maximum investment for your family in the century beyond, or convince the spouse you already have of the need to change your jointly-held, spiritual investment plan with a view to the century beyond.

Then you will want to make sure to reveal this understanding of life to your children and other young people at the earliest reasonable moment. Stimulate their desire to invest in their own life impact. You multiply your influence, generation by generation.

If you understand that you live for what your life will accomplish in others the century after your death, all decisions will be considered in light of the impact that will only be appreciated fully long after the events.

Would I have made different choices—done things differently—if I had known a decade ago, or three, that my life's impact awaited a century of growth in the minds and hearts of others to reach its ultimate influence, reverberating through the lives of children, and grandchildren, both mine and those of people I had spoken to of the Lord's ways? Oh, yes! If I had only realized, I would have invested single-mindedly for maximum results, even though the payoff would not come until a century on.

And how about you? Are you living for today, just for the moment? Or are you living your life to increase your investment and ensure your maximum return on that investment when the words and deeds of a lifetime will reach maturity in the lives of generations to come, generations yet unborn?

Ripple the pond for the century beyond.

৯৩

7.

Abiding in God's Abiding Word

Psalm 119:105 and 11 KJV

*105 "Thy word is a lamp unto my feet,
and a light unto my path."*

*11 "Thy word have I hid in mine heart,
that I might not sin against thee."*

৵৽৻

If you live long enough, most of the things you see and hear
will remind you of something else. I have reached that age. People
I meet look like people I have known. New experiences call to
mind events of long ago. For instance, I watch the bright red
"Children's Church" banner paraded down the aisle each week
with our boys and girls falling in behind and I remember my sense
of excitement as a child when I joined the Vacation Bible School[47]
processionals in my home church. It is a vivid memory for me still.

---

[47] Vacation Bible School (VBS) is a time-honored, Bible-story-focused, summer
program for children held by many churches. In my childhood, VBS might last
for two or three weeks. With most mothers now working outside the home, one
week is the norm—if that is even possible.

Each morning, we were lined up and marched into the sanctuary as the pianist played "Crown Him with Many Crowns."[48] Leading us up the aisles were the sixth-grade boys and girls, carrying the American flag, the Christian flag, and the Bible. And how we longed for the year when it would be our turn to carry them! We were taught pledges to the flags and the Bible, and we recited them every day, year after year.

The pledge to the American Flag, we all know, of course. But I still remember the words to the other pledges, words I first learned at the age of three. The pledge to the Bible went like this:

> "I pledge allegiance to the Bible,
> God's Holy Word.
> I will make it a lamp unto my feet
> and a light unto my path.
> I will hide its words in my heart,
> that I might not sin against God."

Years later, while reading my Bible (and, specifically, Psalm 119), I discovered that, in reciting that pledge, I had been quoting scripture, almost verbatim, as you can see.

୧୦∽

In time, I "aged out" of Vacation Bible School—and thought I had outgrown what they had taught me there. In my adolescent cynicism, I found this homespun pledge rather silly. But I did not forget it. Nor was I able to forget the basic Bible training the good people there gave me.

Oh, I ignored it often enough, when I found it constricting or inconvenient. I rationalized behavior that I knew the Bible opposed. I gladly embraced interpretations of the Bible that eased my conscience, even if they did not reduce my guilt.

The result was predictable. You might even say, "pre-ordained." I suffered, and I hurt other people. I diminished the

---

[48] Matthew Bridges, "Crown Him with Many Crowns," 1851.

Bible's power to shape and nurture me. I damaged my usefulness to the God Who created me and redeemed me—usefulness that the Bible could have supported.

To the degree that I had not honored my childhood pledge, I had proved in the negative its essential truth and value. These words—and the verses they are based on—are not silly. My arrogant assumption that they were, however, was.

Years have passed—many years, and how quickly they go—but the word of God remains. And I have found the Bible to have been for me the dependable constant in a world ever changing. Its words comfort and convict. They bestow blessings and wisdom and power in both the light and the darkness of life. They speak God's word and reveal God's nature and reaffirm God's promises to all who are willing to read the Bible in faith and submission. In the Bible, God comes to commune with His children.

And so, the pledge and its underlying verses seem pretty intelligent today. Let me show you why.

❧

"Thy word is a lamp unto my feet."

What does this mean? The Bible will shed a penetrating light on you. When you read the Bible, you will see yourself as you are, for what you are, the good and the bad. No pretense is possible with God. No pretense is healthy for you. The Bible will not let you deceive yourself about your behavior—or your heart. The Bible will protect you from those who would flatter you or harass you or ridicule you to manipulate you for sinful purposes of their own. Seeing yourself as God sees you can be painful to your ego, but in the Bible's holy light you can become who you were intended to be.

"Thy word...is a light unto my path."

The Bible will also show you the truth about the world around you. It's awfully hard to know what to make of the world these days. Everyone does what is right in his own eyes.[49] All values are considered equally valid. Everything can be justified. "Do what you feel like doing! Make yourself happy!"

But pain and sorrow and anger and want have not gone away in this "do-your-own-thing" world. How do you make sense of life under such conditions? The Bible can show you. Unfortunately, though the Bible remains the best *selling* book of all time, it has become for many a mystery locked away in pages never read. The Bible is no longer the moral and spiritual authority of society that it was in times past, and yet, it still has the world's number cold.

The Bible is God's accurate interpreter of everything under the sun—and everything beyond it. Want to know what things really look like? Direct the light of God's word upon them.

ನ•೦

"I will hide Your word in my heart…"

That, of course, is exactly where God's word belongs. So put it where it belongs and where it can do the most good. In case you haven't noticed, the Bible has enemies—powerful enemies. And since they can't do anything about the Bible—since *"the word of the Lord endures forever"*[50]—the alternative is to separate you from God's word. Hide God's word in your heart so that God's enemies can't separate you from it, and so that it can have its greatest impact upon you and, through you, on others.

That's what Jesus did when He faced temptation in the desert. He wasn't quoting editorials from *The New York Times*—or witty dialogue from *Seinfeld* [51]—when He answered the devil. The Son of God went head to head with the son of perdition and shut him out with scripture He learned as the son of a Jewish carpenter. And so can you, if you do your homework every day. The Bible will

---

[49] Judges 21:25.

[50] 1 Peter 1:25.

[51] A popular and culturally influential television situation comedy starring comedian Jerry Seinfeld and airing from 1989 to 1998.

strengthen you and take care of God's enemies. But you've got to know it and use it. Read it, study it, believe it and trust it.

"*...that I might not sin against God.*"

God has provided His word to enable us to live in right relationship with Him. The word of God shows us sin and reveals to us that God has released us from its evil embrace. The word of God warns us of sin's subtle seductions and protects us from its destructive power. The word of God draws us to the love of God and unfolds for us His will. The Bible is God's word, and we are God's children who were created to hear God's voice and answer in loving obedience and faith.

৯•৬

Today, I reaffirm my allegiance to the Bible, God's holy word. I invite you—I challenge you—to take the pledge with me. I invite you to undertake a life-long relationship with the Bible. Whether you are eight or 18 or 88, I challenge you this day to make a solemn commitment to Almighty God—and to back it up with your action every day—that you will take God's word as your life's guide and authority—that you will read it every day—that you will study it, alone and with other believers, wherever you are and whatever your circumstances—that you will apply the wisdom you find in its pages to every question, thought or deed you consider throughout your life.

Invest in a Bible, if you haven't already—and not just one that will look impressive as it collects dust on a corner table or some out of the way shelf. Buy a Bible you can understand, but one that is faithful to what the writers actually wrote. Put it through its paces. When you wear it out, tape it up or buy another one. The message is sacred, not the paper it's printed on. Mark the passages that inspire you or humble you, and memorize verses you may need in a pinch later on. God may reveal a truth to you years before He plans for you to use it.

Share what you find with others—with Christians and non-Christians, with friends and strangers. If you don't inspire them, you may perplex them, which is the next best thing. As much as Christians need to hear God's word, the lost need to hear it more.

Submit your life to the authority of scripture. Today, most people act as though scripture should be submitted to human authority. If you disagree with something in the Bible, ask yourself "Why?" What is it that you do not know or understand about your world or your circumstances that would cause you to disagree with the Bible? What does God know that you do not? What are you missing?

When you come to the point of assuming that a gap between what the Bible says and what you believe is evidence of some inadequacy in what you believe, you are properly positioned to receive a revelation from God and to grow spiritually as a result.

You do not have to understand its purpose at every point to submit to the Bible's authority. But you will have to submit to its authority to experience its power to transform your life and reveal the presence and will of its divine Author. And a nodding acquaintance with the sacred scriptures of your faith is not enough. The Bible should be your food and drink, your clothing and shelter, your constant companion and your moral compass.

Are you intimidated by the scope of the Bible and how much you do not know about it? Are you starting so late you wonder whether it's worth the effort? Listen, the Bible is God's revelation. God inspired its writing, and He inspires its reading, even by you and me. God will reveal to you what He wants you to know, regardless of how much you don't know. Put God's word where it belongs in your life.

Jesus said, *"If you hold to my teaching, you are really my disciples. Then you will know the truth, and the truth will set you free."*[52]

మత

---

[52] John 8:32-34, NIV.

Psalm 126 NIV

¹ *When the* LORD *restored the fortunes of Zion,*
we were like those who dreamed.
² *Our mouths were filled with laughter,*
our tongues with songs of joy.
Then it was said among the nations,
"The LORD *has done great things for them."*
³ *The* LORD *has done great things for us,*
and we are filled with joy.

⁴ *Restore our fortunes,* LORD,
like streams in the Negev.
⁵ *Those who sow with tears*
will reap with songs of joy.
⁶ *Those who go out weeping,*
carrying seed to sow,
will return with songs of joy,
carrying sheaves with them.

ॐ••ॐ

8.

Restore Our Fortunes

Psalm 126 NIV

Have any of you considered how remarkable it is that we would be provided a psalm to recite today that is really a prayer that God would restore our fortunes? I bought my copy of the lectionary assigning this psalm to this day in 1992. That's 16 years ago! Now I ask you: How did they know?!

"Restore our fortunes, Lord—like streams in the Negev."

Except that there aren't any streams in the Negev—usually. The Negev is the desert that stretches across the southern part of Israel and, most of the time, there's no water there. The streambeds are dry.

But if the rains come—if a storm breaks over the desert—the Negev is transformed, and water flows everywhere, and the desert comes to life. It is immediate. It is massive. It is miraculous. "Restore our fortunes, O Lord, like rivers in the desert."

❧

Just about everybody has lost a fortune of some size or other this year. Those big old nest eggs they used to show everybody carrying around in those investment commercials[53] will probably all fit back in the little egg cartons now. We've talked a lot in our sermons about what we've all lost over the past few months, but this time—this morning—in this passage, it's not about the money. Really.

The fortunes the people of God are praying for are not financial. They're praying about their fate, their destiny, the experiences of their lives as a people that form their identity. When we pray their words, their prayer, we're praying for things far more important than an "up-tick" in the stock market—as nice as that would be. We're praying about the meaning and purpose of our lives, about our relationship with God in this world and the next.

You survived the geography lesson a minute ago. Let's see how you do with a little history.

The psalm begins with the memory of God bringing captives back to Zion, the hill in Jerusalem where the Temple of Solomon was built. The captives in the psalm were the Jewish people taken away to Babylon when their country was conquered and their capital destroyed. And in Babylon they stayed, exiles held captive, for 70 years.

But nations rise and nations fall, and God restores the fortunes of His people. The great Babylon was conquered as little Judah had been. The Jewish people were released from their captivity and allowed to go home. And those who did, entered Jerusalem and climbed Mount Zion in a state of euphoria. The Lord had brought them back to Zion. Against all odds, defying all logic, God had brought them back. The Lord had restored their fortunes.

But not their portfolios. It's ironic: many of the Jews had made a lot of money in Babylon—as exiles. Many of them chose to stay there—with their money and the businesses that made the money.

---

[53] Commercials for A. G. Edwards & Sons, Inc., a financial brokerage firm. The firm sponsored the commercials for several years before they went out of business in 2007.

On the other hand, many of the Jews who undertook the journey back to Jerusalem had little money. And there was even less to be made once they got there.

But they were in Jerusalem—they had returned to Zion out of captivity—and they understood that their fortunes had been restored. They were again in their lives *where* God wanted them to be and *who* God wanted them to be, and they knew that God alone had made it happen.

And the knowledge that God had restored their fortunes left them stunned. How could they have been released from their lifetime of bondage? How could they be standing on holy ground? How could they be so fortunate—so blessed?

Sometimes you experience something so wonderful that you simply can't explain it. If you try to explain it, it just leaves you speechless—like someone in a trance—dreaming. I've seen that look on the faces of little children the instant they see all the presents on Christmas morning.

But what you can't explain, you can celebrate. And when you start to celebrate, the laughter comes. When the Lord brought back the captives to Zion, first they were like men who dreamed—and then their mouths were filled with laughter.

Do you get the picture? Not pleasant smiles or friendly chuckles, but laughter you can't hold back—laughter that spreads your lips so wide that your face almost disappears.

And the joy!

You know, you can have so much joy in your heart that it spreads to your tongue and makes you want to sing so bad that you don't care if you don't know one note from another and couldn't hit the right pitch with a pitch pipe—or a pitching wedge, for that matter.

And people who weren't part of the pilgrimage could tell something had happened to them. Even these people who didn't particularly like them had to admit, based on what they saw, *"The LORD has done great things for them."* You couldn't miss it.

But if you weren't one of the captives God set free, you didn't know the half of it. Nobody knows what it's like to have your fortunes restored by God unless it's happened to you.

And maybe no one knows what it's like to need your fortunes restored by God unless He's restored your fortunes before. God broke the bonds of their captivity. He brought them back to Zion. He gave them something miraculous to celebrate.

But life wasn't all eggnog and mistletoe—even then. Even life in the Holy Land can be hard. Life as the people of God was a constant struggle with everybody else. The people of God didn't always get along with each other, either. And then times got hard. So they prayed.

*"Restore our fortunes, O L*ORD. Life has become so dry and barren. We remember what You did when You brought us to this place. We remember when You set us free. We know You had a divine purpose in that, but that purpose is not yet fulfilled."

"Restore our fortunes," they prayed. "Shower us with Your life-giving power and fulfill Your purpose in redeeming us."

And what does the Lord say?

"Those who sow in tears will reap with songs of joy." Not exactly what you want to hear when you're praying for your basic fortune restoration. You pray a prayer like that and you want to hear something like, "Coming right up!" or "Let the good times roll!" or at least, "Let me think about it and I'll get back to you." Instead, it's *"...sow in tears...reap with...joy."*

Even when God restores the fortunes of His people—even when He takes them out of bondage and returns them from exile—even when God saves people—He sets them in a hard place where they have a job to do. God sets His people in His field, to plant seed in stubborn soil. The work is hard because the soil is so often unyielding. And the sower weeps, knowing that not every seed, precious as it is, will bear fruit.

But the sacrifice and sorrow involved in sowing seed is not God's final answer. The present sacrifice, offered by the people of

God in memory of His first great work to restore their fortunes, is also offered in hope of the great work that is to come: the joyful harvest.

They prayed about Babylon and Zion, about conquest and captivity and coming back to the Land of Promise. And when we, as Christians, pray for the restoration of our fortunes, what are we praying for? We have not been held prisoner in Babylon or released to the land of our ancestors. Our captivity has been to sin and our coming back is to the bosom of God the Father. Our eternal fortunes were restored when a Child born in holiness and humility grew to manhood, and died in sacrificial agony, as God intended.

And in that holy Child—that special Man—God broke the bonds of our captivity to sin and death. He brought us back to the Zion of His heart. He gave us something miraculous to celebrate. As so we laugh for joy and sing at the birth of our Messiah.

But the life of the Christian is still hard. We await the fulfillment of the promise of redemption amid the frustration of a world still given over to sin and death.

And rather than relishing our eternal reward in heaven, we remain rooted in this world, struggling to sow the seeds of the gospel, weeping over all that undermines our success, in the world, and in us.

We have known the restoration of our fortunes in the grace of our God. We celebrate Christmas with wonder, laughter and song. We know, even now, the hardships of life in the Lord, even at Christmas time. We sow each day the seeds of salvation, weeping to see the world in its fallenness around us, weeping to see the opposition it raises to our work.

But we await the final restoration of our fortunes as Christians, when the weeping of the present—the sorrows and sacrifices of each day—will give way to the joyful song of heaven's harvest, and the Christ Who came…will come again.

> *"When the* LORD *restored the fortunes of Zion,*
>   *we were like those who dream.*
> *Then our mouth was filled with laughter,*
>   *and our tongues with shouts of joy."*

Restore our fortunes again, O Lord.
Restore our fortunes again.

☞☜

From the Book of Isaiah

Isaiah 6:1-13 ESV

[1] *In the year that King Uzziah died I saw the* Lord *sitting upon a throne, high and lifted up; and the train of his robe filled the temple.* [2] *Above him stood the seraphim. Each had six wings: with two he covered his face, and with two he covered his feet, and with two he flew.* [3] *And one called to another and said:*

> *"Holy, holy, holy is the* LORD *of hosts;*
> *the whole earth is full of his glory!"*

[4] *And the foundations of the thresholds shook at the voice of him who called, and the house was filled with smoke.* [5] *And I said: "Woe is me! For I am lost; for I am a man of unclean lips, and I dwell in the midst of a people of unclean lips; for my eyes have seen the King, the* LORD *of hosts!"*

[6] *Then one of the seraphim flew to me, having in his hand a burning coal that he had taken with tongs from the altar.* [7] *And he touched my mouth and said: "Behold, this has touched your lips; your guilt is taken away, and your sin atoned for."*

[8] *And I heard the voice of the Lord saying, "Whom shall I send, and who will go for us?" Then I said, "Here I am! Send me."* [9] *And he said, "Go, and say to this people:*

> *"'Keep on hearing, but do not understand;*
> *keep on seeing, but do not perceive.'*
> [10] *Make the heart of this people dull,*
>   *and their ears heavy,*
>   *and blind their eyes;*
> *lest they see with their eyes,*
>   *and hear with their ears,*
> *and understand with their hearts,*
>   *and turn and be healed."*
> [11] *Then I said, "How long, O Lord?"*

And he said:
"Until cities lie waste without inhabitant,
   and houses without people,
   and the land is a desolate waste,
[12] *and the* LORD *removes people far away,*
   and the forsaken places
   are many in the midst of the land.
[13] *And though a tenth remain in it,*
   it will be burned again,
   like a terebinth or an oak,
   whose stump remains
   when it is felled."
The holy seed is its stump.

 formative

Revelation 4:1-11 ESV

[1] *After this I looked, and behold, a door standing open in heaven! And the first voice, which I had heard speaking to me like a trumpet, said, "Come up here, and I will show you what must take place after this."* [2] *At once I was in the Spirit, and behold, a throne stood in heaven, with one seated on the throne.* [3] *And he who sat there had the appearance of jasper and carnelian, and around the throne was a rainbow that had the appearance of an emerald.* [4] *Around the throne were twenty-four thrones, and seated on the thrones were twenty-four elders, clothed in white garments, with golden crowns on their heads.* [5] *From the throne came flashes of lightning, and rumblings and peals of thunder, and before the throne were burning seven torches of fire, which are the seven spirits of God,* [6] *and before the throne there was as it were a sea of glass, like crystal.*

And around the throne, on each side of the throne, are four living creatures, full of eyes in front and behind: [7] *the first living creature like a lion, the second living creature like an ox, the third living creature with the face of a man, and the fourth living creature like an eagle in flight.* [8] *And the four living creatures, each of them with six wings, are full of eyes all around and within, and day and night they never cease to say,*

> *"Holy, holy, holy, is the Lord God Almighty,*
> *who was and is and is to come!"*

[9] *And whenever the living creatures give glory and honor and thanks to him who is seated on the throne, who lives forever and ever,* [10] *the twenty-four elders fall down before him who is seated on the throne and worship him who lives forever and ever. They cast their crowns before the throne, saying,*

> [11] *"Worthy are you, our Lord and God,*
> *to receive glory and honor and power,*
> *for you created all things,*
> *and by your will they existed and were created."*

∂∽◦

9.

On Earth as It Is in Heaven

Isaiah 6:1-13; Revelation 4:1-11 ESV

Sometimes, God gives you a glimpse of heaven. Maybe, like Isaiah, you show up one day in the place you always go to worship, and everything is the same—except nothing is the same, because, this time, you don't see the same old stuff—you don't see what everybody else is seeing—you see God, seated on His throne, high and lifted up—God in His awesome glory and terrifying holiness. And what you see scares the hell out of you because seeing God—even a little bit of God in all His heavenly majesty—will do that, because, if you can see God, you know He can see you.

Or maybe, like John, you're sitting around nowhere special and for some reason—or no reason—whatever was on your mind is replaced by a sudden sense of something your mind can't get itself around, and yet there it is: heaven—and not just pretty clouds and rays of sunlight. You see and sense a place so beautiful and spectacular and unlike this world that you know it's not this world or any part of it. It's so beautiful and so spectacular that it scares you because you know you're not supposed to be there—to be seeing what you're seeing—even though you've never wanted to be anywhere so much as you want to be there.

Sometimes, God gives you a glimpse of heaven. But what God shows you is not the place, but Himself *in* the place: God in context. You see, there is no heaven without God, and because there is God, there is heaven, too. There can't *not* be.

Heaven is what emanates from and surrounds the divine, eternal, infinite God, the Creator and Sustainer of all that is, the Understander of all that has been and will be, and the Purpose for which all things are. When we pray, *"Our Father, Who art in heaven,"*[54] we are not suggesting that God is in heaven as opposed to, say, Cleveland, or China, or Mars, or some other point in space, near or far. God is in heaven because heaven is what naturally and necessarily attaches itself to a Being—a Reality—as unlimitedly powerful and breathtakingly holy as God. Where God is, there is heaven around Him.

And where God goes, heaven goes with Him—which is why we can pray, *"Thy kingdom come—Thy will be done—on earth as it is in heaven."* We ask God to come here, to earth, to us, to our situations and circumstances—and if He does—when He does—heaven comes with Him.

That is why there can be, and is, the sense of the divine in what seems like the most ungodly of places. That's why a godly home feels like heaven, even if there is nothing else there. That's why time spent in the company of a devout Christian is so heavenly: God is there—and heaven with Him—in His relationship with that person. It's why when Jacob woke up from a dream about a stairway to heaven he exclaimed, *"The LORD is in this place and I did not know it."*[55]

Jesus went about telling people, *"...the kingdom of heaven is at hand"*[56]—is here—because Jesus was the Incarnation of God—God come to earth in the Person and Life of Jesus,[57] bringing

---

54 Matthew 6:9, RSV.
55 Genesis 28:16, RSV.
56 Matthew 4:17, ESV.
57 Philippians 2:6-7.

heaven with Him.[58] It's this same Jesus, now risen from the dead and ascended into heaven[59]—into the fullness of the divinity of God's Being[60]—Who speaks to John in the Book of Revelation[61] and gives John a glimpse of heaven—letting John see what the human eye seldom sees even though it is always there, nonetheless: the overwhelming glory and splendor that flows from—and follows—God.

What Isaiah saw and what John saw sound very much like the same thing, though John offers more description. What Isaiah saw was a vision of heaven revealed within the Jerusalem Temple, in the mysterious Holy of Holies, a place where long before the birth of Jesus, God promised His people He would choose[62] for the "joy of heaven to earth come down."[63]

And amid the sights and smells and sounds of worship, what Isaiah saw and heard made him feel the fear of the very presence of God. God pulled back the veil of physical limitation and showed Isaiah what was just beyond the curtain of human experience and awareness: the kingdom of God was at hand—for *him*.

In each case, Isaiah and John discover that heaven is where God is Sovereign—where He is King—undisputed, unchallenged, unrestricted Ruler. They see God, but not so much in detail as in impression. As much as anything, they see the impact of God, the effect His very presence has on what is around Him, and how those supernatural beings who attend Him respond to Him.

Isaiah and John see power and splendor, magnitude and majesty. They hear unceasing praise and proclamation of God's identity, nature and accomplishments.

The difference between earth and heaven, then, is more about our being unwilling, in this world, fallen as it is into (and because

---

[58] Colossians 1:19.
[59] Ephesians 1:20.
[60] Hebrews 1:3.
[61] Revelation 1:17-18.
[62] Deuteronomy 12:5.
[63] From Charles Wesley, "Love Divine, All Loves Excelling," Stanza 1, 1747.

of) sin, to acknowledge and submit to and rejoice in the infinite and righteous sovereignty of God over us and all He has created, which is everything. Here on earth, we dispute and challenge God's rule. We try to restrict God's authority and power in our lives and our society. We do not see the grandeur of heaven because we are unwilling to believe it exists, because to do so would require us to believe in and submit to a Sovereign God.

God reveals many things to many people, but He seldom reveals the overwhelming wonder and glory of heaven to those who are determined not to see any part of heaven even when they're looking right at it.

In the last few weeks, huge billboards went up in the Charlotte area proclaiming the fervent faith of a group calling itself American Atheists: "God is sadistic, and Jesus Christ is useless as a Savior."

Are they likely to see the Lord of Hosts, the Lord God Almighty, seated on His heavenly throne, high and lifted up? No, not likely—not before Judgment Day, anyway, (and then only briefly, I suspect).

But *you* might catch a glimpse of heaven someday. You may already have. You may have had that encounter with God that opened a window on heaven for you. You may have seen something that you could not imagine and cannot describe, and yet there it was and there you were and that's all there is to it.

What did little three-year-old Colton Burpo say after waking from a near-death experience? "Heaven is for real!"[64] He had been there and seen it—which should be no surprise since Jesus said, *"...unless you change and become like little children, you will never enter the kingdom of heaven"*[65] (or even see it, probably).

But if you could see heaven—if you could see the amazing wonder and incredible majesty and breathtaking beauty and

---

[64] Todd Burpo and Lynn Vincent, *Heaven is for Real: A Little Boy's Astounding Story of His Trip to Heaven and Back,* New York: Thomas Nelson, 2010.
[65] Matthew 18:3, NIV.

terrifying power that make up the reality that surrounds and flows from God, what would you do?

I'm not talking about going to heaven at the end of this earthly life when, as Paul says, the perishable is raised imperishable, in glory and power, and what is now mortal becomes immortal.[66] Yes, if you believe in Jesus, you're going to heaven for all eternity[67] because you've been promised a place there[68] and that's where you will belong.

But what about before then—before you go to heaven—when God brings heaven to you?

Isaiah saw God in His heavenly glory in the year that King Uzziah died—in the years leading up to the destruction of his country. John saw the heavenly throne room of God when churches were being persecuted and Christians were being martyred and John himself was an exile for his faith on an out-of-the-way island. Servants of God seem to see heaven most often when things aren't going so well for them and God's people on earth—when times are hard, and the temptation is high to cut a deal with the world to give up on God and go along with everybody else. God seems to give you a glimpse of heaven most often when what you see on earth doesn't look anything like heaven.

And why?

Because God wants you to know that heaven and earth aren't that much different, as far as He is concerned. They're both His.

Catch a glimpse of heaven with God on His celestial throne ruling over all that is natural and supernatural with absolute authority and matchless splendor—see the realm where no creature or power disputes, challenges, or wants (or attempts) to restrict God's sovereignty—and you see what this earth is not yet, but one day will be.

---

[66] 1 Corinthians 15:42-54.
[67] 1 Thessalonians 4:16-17.
[68] John 14:3.

One day, this world and all that is in it will understand, welcome, and do the will of God—as fully, faithfully and joyfully as the saints and seraphim gathered around God do now. All in this world will bow and confess His Lordship, just as all above and below the earth do now.[69]

All will proclaim God holy—and worthy to receive every honor. All will cast their crowns or whatever they possess and treasure at His feet. All will see heaven in all its God-reflecting glory, and the earth the same way, because, as the prophet Habakkuk says,

> *"...the earth will be filled*
> *with the knowledge of the glory of the LORD,*
> *as the waters cover the sea."*[70]

You see, "this is my Father's world"—this earth. And if He provides you a glimpse of heaven while you're here, it is to remind you that

> "...though the wrong seems oft so strong,
> God is the Ruler yet."

The kingdom of heaven is submissive to its Sovereign while the earth remains, for now, in rebellion. But

> "...the battle is not done.
> Jesus Who died shall be satisfied,
> and earth and heaven shall be one"[71]

all under the rule of God.

To see heaven—to see God in His "context"—while we are here on earth—is to see the answer to our prayers, not just about where we will go when we die, but that where we are now, this earth, will also be redeemed and restored to the kingdom of God, and will be obedient to the will of God.[72]

---

[69] Philippians 2:11.
[70] Habakkuk 2:14, RSV.
[71] Maltbie D. Babcock, "This is My Father's World," 1901.
[72] Romans 8:19-22.

Can you see it? His kingdom come—His will done—on earth as it is in heaven.[73]

Glory halleluiah! What a vision!

❧

---

[73] Matthew 6:10.

.

10.

When the Leader is Gone

Isaiah 6:1-13 ESV (pp. 66-67)

Changing leaders is always a traumatic experience. It is traumatic because so much is at stake for so many people, and because so much about the future is simply unknown. Of course, it's a lot easier to deal with when the transition is orderly, and we know exactly how and when everything will take place. But we're not always that lucky.

I started reading a copy of Harry Truman's memoirs[74] not long ago. He begins by talking about the loss of President Franklin Roosevelt in April of 1945. Roosevelt had been president for 12 of the most difficult years in American history, from the depths of the Great Depression to the waning days of World War II. He had brought hope and confidence and vision to the nation and the world. He had been the only president most children had ever known.

When the train brought his body back from Warm Springs, Georgia, to Washington, D.C., thousands of people, many in tears, gathered day and night at every stop along the route. Truman said

---

[74] Harry S. Truman, *Memoirs: Year of Decisions*, Garden City, NY: Doubleday, 1955.

he "felt like the moon, the stars, and all the planets had fallen on" him. The nation's leader was gone.

And though he has not died, a great leader of this church is also gone.[75] You knew he was going, but you do not know who or what this period of transition will bring, or even how long it will last. And for the hope and confidence and vision he provided many of you throughout the years, in times, perhaps, of hardship or conflict, his going is a heavy blow. You may be afraid, like many were in 1945, that the new man may not "have what it takes" to fill the leader's shoes.

This is the context of your church today. It's one of the most significant things you bring with you to worship. Now, you don't even know what's going to happen in the worship service each week. It won't be as predictable as it used to be. It may not be as comfortable an experience. There may be unexpected and unpleasant surprises. And there may be something else.

There may be the Lord, high and lifted up.

You see, this is God's church. Your pastor was only an "under-shepherd." Your next pastor will be no more. God is your true Leader, now and always. And do you think that God does not know what you are feeling and what you are needing? Do you think that God does not have a plan to meet your needs in a pastor as in everything else? Or do you think that God does not have the ability to carry His plan to its proper completion?

Jesus said to His disciples, *"I will not leave you as orphans; I will come to you."*[76]

So what do you do when the leader is gone?

Perhaps we can find some answers to that question in Isaiah, Chapter 6.

బ్‌•ళ

---

[75] I had been asked to preach for a Baptist church whose pastor of some 30 years had recently retired. In the Baptist system, pastors are called by the local congregation after a search process; they are not appointed as in other systems.

[76] John 14:18, ESV.

Isaiah does several things in this critical time when a great leader is gone. First, he seeks God. When their earthly leader is gone, Isaiah goes to the Temple, the earthly house of his heavenly Leader. Out in the world, you may discover and enjoy the breathtaking evidence of God's creativity. You may be inspired by a walk in the woods or one on the golf course, by seeing a sunrise at your favorite fishing hole or by missing one at "Bedsprings Baptist." Out in the world, you can find the wonder of God's creation. Even the seraphim acknowledge that: *"The whole earth is full of His glory!"* But the house of God is the place to look for the Creator of the world Himself.

When your earthly leader—your under-shepherd—is gone, you need God more. The question is, "Will you seek Him more— or less?" Will you exercise the discipline necessary to put yourself in the place and the perspective where your chance of a genuine encounter with God is greatest? Or will you instead allow yourself to be depressed and distracted from spiritual things just because that familiar face—that familiar voice and manner—are not here to challenge you to maintain your proper commitment to your God and your church?

ঙ•৩

When the leader is gone, you must look upward. The Psalmist said, *"I will lift up mine eyes unto the hills from whence cometh my help. My help cometh from the LORD!"*[77]

Isaiah not only seeks God, Isaiah sees Him. *"In the year that King Uzziah died, I saw the Lord, sitting upon a throne, high and lifted up; and His train filled the temple."*

In this same book, the call goes out, *"Seek the LORD while He may be found."*[78] This is a God Who has chosen to appear to those who seek Him. Our God is a revealing God. He lets us see His

---

[77] Psalm 121:1-2, KJV.
[78] Isaiah 55:7, RSV.

glory. He lets us hear His word. He lets us understand His nature and His purpose.

Where do people see God but in places like this? Isaiah had been to thousands of worship services. What makes this one different? Who knows? But it is. In the midst of worship—amid the familiar setting and activities—Isaiah sees what everybody else sees—but he sees more. In this moment, amid all these people, Isaiah finds himself alone with God—alone before God. Isaiah has become aware of the divine reality behind the human ritual, which is the purpose in all our rituals—all the religious things we do. In a critical time of transition, Isaiah has become more sensitive to the spiritual—the eternal—realities.

The women in my family are exceptionally talented musicians. They not only know how to play well, they also have a better ear for the quality of the sound their instruments produce. While I always think that what I hear is wonderful, they are not so easily satisfied. If they hear a discord, it must be corrected. Their music is beautiful because they are more sensitive to pitch and tone and harmony. When the leader is gone, those who are left must "fine tune" their spiritual perception so that in seeking God, they may see Him—and see Him as He is.

This is a time for you to see God, to see Him as He truly is, to see Him high and lifted up, to see His holiness and His glory. Your leader is gone. Look upward. Seek God.

৯৯৯

Of course, Isaiah doesn't just see the Lord. Isaiah sees the Lord Who sees Isaiah. We're not talking here about the giddy excitement of catching a glimpse of somebody famous from a safe distance. We're talking about a real "in-your-face" encounter with a holy and powerful God, from Whom there is no place to hide.

When the leader is gone, in addition to looking upward and seeing God, you need to look inward and see yourself.

The contrast can be painful—and terrifying. The piercing light of God's holiness reveals Isaiah's sinful nature, a nature that cannot be hidden from Him. Isaiah sees himself in God's holy light, and he does the only thing he can do. He confesses his sin and awaits the response of God.

And God's response is an amazing grace. God forgives. God redeems. God purifies the unclean lips. His realization of his sin creates in Isaiah an overwhelming sense of unworthiness. He humbles himself before God. When you see God accurately, the result will be to see yourself accurately as well. To see yourself as accurately as God sees you is always a humbling experience. And in that humility, that emptying yourself of ego and pride, God finds room to implant His Holy Spirit and work His will.

God can do something with us when we see what we are before Him and know our need. But only when we have recognized our sin and have been set free from it can we do the will of God. When the leader is gone, take a good, hard, honest look inside. See yourself as God sees you and respond accordingly.

Look upward. Look inward. Seek God and see yourself.

୧୭

Then look outward.

When the leader is gone, God calls us to be His messengers to the *"people of unclean lips."* The purification of Isaiah prepares him for God's purpose. You see, neither God's revelation nor our redemption is an end in itself. Isaiah understands that the spiritual vision, the forgiveness and the consecration are to equip him to serve, to do God's will and to speak His word. And so it is with us.

When the leader is gone, God is near. Seek Him in His house.

When the leader is gone, God illuminates our lives. See yourself and your need and receive His grace.

When the leader is gone, God calls us to a ministry of word and deed. Serve His people, in and beyond this fellowship.

Somewhere, God is preparing a new leader for you. In fact, God has been preparing that leader for a long time—perhaps all his life. It is only right that you let God prepare you for the coming of that new leader He will provide you.

੩•੬

11.

In the Presence of the Lord

Isaiah 6:1-13 ESV (pp. 66-67)

In a quiet room, a man sits at a table alone. He dips a pen in ink and begins to write: *"In the year that King Uzziah died, I saw the Lord…"* He pauses—remembering—then more words flow from his pen. The room is quiet, but the man's mind and heart are not.

The man is well-known in his community. He travels in the highest circles of government and society. But he is not popular. He has criticized the rich and powerful. He has predicted disaster for the whole country.

But they have not believed him. They have done the exact opposite of what he told them to do. And he has suffered the consequences that come to those who tell important people what they do not want to hear. They have condemned him as disloyal and defeatist. By their measure, he is narrow and intolerant on matters of morals and religion—attitudes they refuse to tolerate.

And so finally, he sits down and puts down in writing the explanation for his actions. "I have said what I have said—I have done what I have done—because, in the year that King Uzziah died, I saw the Lord—and in the process of that encounter, the Lord sent me to say what I have said, and to do what I have done."

The man at the table is Isaiah, known to us as the Prince of Prophets. But to his contemporaries, he was Isaiah, the royal pain in the neck. The only reason we know him today—that we find the explanation he wrote in our Bibles—is that what he said came true, and what he did accurately demonstrated what was to become of the country whose leaders chose to ignore the God Who brought them into existence. Isaiah was right, in the end, about what would happen if the country's leaders rejected the moral, spiritual and political guidance this God provided.

Things had been different under King Uzziah. Isaiah had grown up under the long rule of Uzziah. Uzziah had been a good king, strong on defense and strong on the economy. There had been peace and prosperity under Uzziah.

But Uzziah had become ill in his later years, and his son had taken over the government. By the time Uzziah died, the golden age of Judah seemed to be over, and great dangers could be seen gathering on the horizon. Foreign countries were building up their military might and making belligerent threats. In response, freedom was traded away for the illusion of security. Domestically, the shapers of popular culture had grown indifferent or hostile to the religious beliefs and practices that were the form and fiber of the people's historic relationship with God.

And one day, in the midst of all that, Isaiah saw the Lord, regal in His demeanor, awesome in His power, holy in His nature.

Why did Isaiah see the Lord? One answer is that the Lord wanted to be seen. If He had not, no one could have seen Him— not Isaiah, not anybody. That's why we sing

> "Immortal, invisible, God only wise,
> in light inaccessible hid from our eyes."[79]

We can only see God when God wants us to see Him and allows us to see Him. The Lord *allowed* Isaiah to see Him. More

---

[79] Walter C. Smith, "Immortal, Invisible, God Only Wise," 1867.

than that, God *enabled* Isaiah to see Him. We may even go so far as to say that God *caused* Isaiah to see Him.

Was Isaiah looking for God? Isaiah does not say, one way or the other. But if he was, Isaiah certainly got a whole lot more than he bargained for when he went looking. What he saw awed him and terrified him, because when Isaiah saw the Lord, he also saw himself in comparison, and the contrast almost scared Isaiah to death.

Was Isaiah looking for God? Isaiah's vision of God may have taken place when Isaiah was in the Temple—the sanctuary of God. Wherever he was, Isaiah saw God in that context, in the great Jerusalem Temple, the holiest place on earth—and yet a place that could not begin to hold the divine power and glory of God that filled it.

Wherever Isaiah was, he was clearly focused on God in a way that the country's leaders were not. And as Isaiah's prophetic colleague Jeremiah would write a century and a half later,

> *"...when you seek me with all your heart,*
> *I will be found by you, says the LORD...."*[80]

The leaders of the country were not looking for God and so they did not see God. God appeared to one who was looking for Him—or was, at least, willing to see Him. And God gave that one a message for those who were not.

But before God could give Isaiah the message, something had to be done about Isaiah—and Isaiah knew it.

Isaiah didn't know yet exactly what God had in store for his country, but Isaiah did recognize what he had to look forward to if his own life didn't change. When Isaiah got a good look at God, he recognized how much of his culture's corruption had seeped into him. And all Isaiah could do in the presence of God was to agree with God about his sinful, defiled condition. Isaiah quickly, completely and contritely confessed himself.

---

[80] Jeremiah 29:13-14, RSV.

And it was enough.

If you find yourself in the presence of God, you will immediately recognize your unworthiness. But you will also find that God can and will take away your unworthiness. God will purify you and sanctify you—if you will allow Him to. The truth, of course, is that we are all in the presence of God—always and everywhere. Those who refuse to believe this—who refuse to recognize this to be true—are still every bit as much in the presence of God as those who, like Isaiah, "see the Lord...high and lifted up."

And those who remain in the presence of God without confession—uncleansed, unpurified, unworthy—will ultimately suffer the fate that Isaiah was finally commissioned to announce to the leaders of his country: Judgment! Doom!

But because of Isaiah's confession, *his* fate was different: The burning coal touched Isaiah's unclean lips and his sin and guilt were blotted out.

And then he heard the Lord's question: *"Whom shall I send?"*

But God is not sending kind souls to feed the hungry and heal the sick and pour out divine benevolence this time. When Isaiah sees God, God has just decided to impose His divine judgment on Isaiah's country—and He has decided to send someone to tell them so. Isaiah is the one God is sending to deliver His message of doom.

Not a call to repentance, understand, but an announcement of the decision God has already reached to punish the people for turning away from Him. And the leaders will no more receive the message of Isaiah than they will accept the love and grace and guidance of God Himself. Their hostile, hardening reaction to Isaiah and his message merely confirms the justice of God's decision.

And so, awash in their misguided hostility, burdened by the awareness of the already unfolding judgment of God, Isaiah sits and writes an explanation of why he will not go along with the popular approach—why he criticizes the policies and practices of those in power—why he paints a picture of an unavoidable destruction to come.

But he will not convince them—he will not change their minds—and he knows it. They will not believe Isaiah when he speaks.

But when the tidal wave of God's wrath has passed over, and the survivors assess the damage and seek a meaning in what has happened, there will be the words of a man who saw the Lord and spoke as the Lord directed. And they will know why they suffered as they did—and what they will need to do differently to avoid suffering that way again.

This is all history, of course: words written in the ancient past—events buried in the forgotten grave of time. Isaiah is long gone and has nothing to tell us today—nothing, that is, unless we in our day, like those in his, are living still in the presence of the Lord. If we are, we will ignore the words of Isaiah at great peril.

If the Lord is not "history"—not an irrelevant fantasy of the past—then look up and see the eternal Lord. The great Temple in Jerusalem is gone, but the Lord still wants and enables you to see Him, high and lifted up—lifted up on a Cross. And He will still cleanse your uncleanness, not with burning coals, but with His own shed blood. And He is still sending His messengers, to this and every nation, so that *"everyone who believes in Him may not perish but have eternal life."*[81]

Look up and see the eternal Lord. Listen up and hear His timeless Word. Wise up and live—live according to His perfect and unchanging will.

කෙ∘ල

---

[81] John 3:16, RSV.

Isaiah 40:27-29 NRSV

[27] *Why do you say, O Jacob,*
  and speak, O Israel,
"My way is hidden from the LORD,
  and my right is disregarded by my God"?
[28] *Have you not known? Have you not heard?*
The LORD *is the everlasting God,*
  the Creator of the ends of the earth.
He does not faint or grow weary;
  his understanding is unsearchable.
[29] *He gives power to the faint,*
  and strengthens the powerless.

ॐॐ

12.

The Everlasting God

Isaiah 40:27-29 NRSV

It has been six weeks or so since we dismantled the organ and displaced the pews in our sanctuary next door to allow the workmen to make repairs. And we are eager to return to our beloved place of worship before too many more days have passed.

But suppose instead of a temporary renovation, our entire church had been completely destroyed. Suppose an enemy army, too strong for us to oppose, had come and burned our sanctuary to the ground, and then forced us out of our homes. And suppose that instead of six weeks, it had been six decades since we had last sat in those pews and listened to the inspiring music and offered our prayers together in that sacred place.

Impossible? Here and now, certainly. But there are those in this room who have experienced the invasion of foreign armies and the destruction of their cities. They know what it is like to lose their homes. There are people here today who have seen everything safe and familiar disappear before their eyes, with not a clue what the next day would bring.

When you have "been there"—in real life or your imagination—you will understand the experience and the perspective of the people to whom Isaiah speaks. They are citizens of a country that no longer exists—men and women and children in exile. Many of these people were born in exile. They have lived all their lives in subjection to foreign masters, cut off from the land of their ancestors and their heritage.

It has been 60 years since their nation was conquered—60 years since their king was dethroned, their capital was demolished, and their sacred site defiled. Sixty years—a lifetime—has passed, and nothing has changed. They remain in exile: no country, no king, no capital, no Temple, the house of their God.

And what of the God they had worshipped in that house?

Day after day, decade after decade, they watch in their exile as other people prosper and other gods are praised for the ongoing prosperity those other people enjoy and the unchallenged power they exert in the world. Was the God of these exiled people defeated and dethroned by the gods of the people who had defeated them? What had become of the God of these exiles?

It seems like a good question—a fair question—for a people who have gone through what they have. What has become of the exiles' God? Is it time for them to trade gods? After all, there are many gods. Families, clans and kingdoms all claim different ones. Given their circumstances, do these exiles need a better god?

You can understand why people, individually and nationally, would go "god-shopping" when their god doesn't do what they want a god to do. If your god is not preventing bad things—if your god is not providing good things—you might just think your god is not doing his job.

And that's what the exiles are saying: "Why do You hide Your face? Why do You forget our affliction and oppression?"

What they mean is: "What good are You to us? Why are You not doing what we want You to do? Don't You know what we want? Are You unwilling or unable to do it? Perhaps we should give up on You and look for a god that is more attentive to us."

That's what you wonder—if your life experience defines your God: Bad life? Bad god.

But just as the exiles' pity party is revving up to a fever pitch, somebody pulls the plug. One man stands up and challenges this whole perspective: "Why are you complaining about the performance of your God? Why are you accusing your God of not doing His job?"

One man, himself an exile, will have none of this griping at, or giving up on, God. He will have none of it—because of who they are—and Who their God is.

"Why do you say, O Jacob? and speak, O Israel?"

The kingdom of Israel is no more, but before Israel was a nation, it was a people—a family. And it remains so. Even in exile, they are the children of Israel.

They are all descendants of a founder, one man, Jacob. And this Jacob became Israel in the course of his lifelong relationship with his God—one particular and unique God amid all the deities claimed by all the other people in the world. And as other gods came and went according to the fate of their followers, the relationship between this Jacob—this Israel—and his God lived on after his death in the lives of his children and their children and theirs. The relationship endured because the descendants of Jacob became Israel and, generation after generation, they reaffirmed his unique relationship with this unique God and made the relationship their own.

❧⋅❧

And a unique thing happened.

These people—these descendants of Jacob—this family Israel—came to believe that this God—their God—defined the meaning of their fate—their experience in the world—while for everybody else, their human fate was the measure of their gods.

And so, for centuries, whether in bondage or in peace and prosperity, the children of Israel had been sustained and preserved as a people by maintaining their relationship with this God.

But commitment to this God is not an automatic thing. Each new generation of Jacob's descendants must choose to embrace the covenant relationship with this God. Every son and daughter of Israel is confronted with the decision to accept this God—and enter into the heritage of the relationship—or not.

And here is a generation of Israel in exile. How do you follow in the spiritual footsteps of your fathers and mothers when the tracks all seem to lead to a lifetime of destruction and despair? How do you proclaim the sovereignty of your God when all the earthly evidence seems to deny it? Isaiah says, "If you have a relationship with a God Who defines the meaning of what happens in your life, you ask a very different question. You challenge the worldly assumptions and popular calculations."

"You are Jacob," Isaiah says, "you are Israel. You are different, and your God is different. You don't have a god; your God has you. Through good times and bad, the first Israel, and every generation of Israel that has followed, has belonged to this God. What happens to you happens within your relationship with this God—and for the (sometimes unfathomable, sometimes foretold) purpose of this God—for you who have acknowledged that you are His.

"Don't you know who you are? It's understandable why someone else would give up on some other god. But you are Jacob—you are Israel—and this is the Lord."

And, of course, when Isaiah says, "the Lord," he means the God of Israel, Whose Name is known, but too sacred and powerful to risk writing it on paper or speaking it aloud.

"Your God," Isaiah says, "is not *a* god; Your God is *THE* God. The God of the patriarch Jacob—the God of the people Israel—is not merely a personal, or even a national, god. Your God is everything He has ever been to you and your ancestors—and He is also the everlasting, eternal God, unlimited in time and space. He is the Creator of all things in existence—He is infinite in power and ability. He is knowledge and wisdom without exception. There is nothing He cannot know or understand. And He is the God—the only God—Who gives power and strength to those who need it."

So do not ask what your adversity tells you about your God; ask what your God will reveal to you about and through your adversity.[82]

Israel is debating whether to give up on their God just as their God is raising up new empires and shattering old ones to end their exile and take them home. They are not in exile because their God is not able to protect them. They are there because they have been unfaithful to their God. And their God—the everlasting, omnipotent, Creator-of-the-universe God—in order to redeem and reform the relationship He established with them—so that they can remain His people—is using the nations of the world—nations He also controls—to punish and purify them—His people—His Israel.

Have you not known—from your own experience—from your own personal sense of relationship with God? Have you not heard—from your parents and your religious leaders, from your sacred scriptures, the laws and prophecies and psalms of your heritage? How did you, the people of Israel, the descendants of Jacob, miss the fact that your God has not only shown you faithfulness and love and grace and mercy, but has demonstrated Himself to be, as well, the one and only everlasting God, infinite in power and wisdom?

The graveyard of gods is full of deities that didn't measure up to the desires of their devotees. And history is cluttered with peoples and nations that raised themselves up for a time in the name of those gods, only to fall back into oblivion, taking their ultimately powerless gods with them.

But Israel, exiled and helpless, weary and despairing, trusts in a proven God, intimately personal and infinitely powerful. And

---

[82] To paraphrase the most famous line from John Kennedy's 1961 inauguration address.

Israel goes home from exile, not to become a great and powerful nation, but to become a bright and shining witness to a great and powerful God.

Israel survives through centuries of hardship and hostility, and becomes the seedbed for a Savior of the world their God created and chose to redeem. And in this Savior, from Israel, and for Israel and all the world, is this God Himself, come to give hope to the faint and power to the powerless.

And you, who have chosen to become the spiritual descendants of Jacob, the new Israel of the everlasting God through the blood of Jesus Christ—do you know that your difficulties, your sorrows, your pain and your fears are not the measure of your God's power or will? Do you see that it is your God—this infinite, timeless, limitless God—Who decides the meaning of your life and what you experience in it? Exiled or exalted, you belong to Him, and He, all-powerful, will give you strength.

ॐॐ

Isaiah 42:1-9 ESV

¹ *Behold my servant, whom I uphold,*
my chosen, in whom my soul delights;
I have put my Spirit upon him;
he will bring forth justice to the nations.
² *He will not cry aloud or lift up his voice,*
or make it heard in the street;
³ *a bruised reed he will not break,*
and a faintly burning wick he will not quench;
he will faithfully bring forth justice.
⁴ *He will not grow faint or be discouraged*
till he has established justice in the earth;
and the coastlands wait for his law.
⁵ *Thus says God, the* LORD,
who created the heavens and stretched them out,
who spread out the earth and what comes from it,
who gives breath to the people on it
and spirit to those who walk in it:
⁶ *"I am the* LORD; *I have called you in righteousness;*
I will take you by the hand and keep you;
I will give you as a covenant for the people,
a light for the nations,
⁷ *to open the eyes that are blind,*
to bring out the prisoners from the dungeon,
from the prison those who sit in darkness.
⁸ *I am the* LORD; *that is my name;*
my glory I give to no other,
nor my praise to carved idols.

⁹ *Behold, the former things have come to pass,*
and new things I now declare;
before they spring forth
I tell you of them."

❧∘❧

13.

A Chosen Servant

Isaiah 42:1-9 ESV

God wants to introduce you to somebody—or perhaps it would be more accurate to say God wants to introduce somebody to you. But it's an odd sort of introduction because you don't get the name. And it's not because you weren't listening, or the name is too hard to pronounce.

God is introducing somebody, but He isn't giving you that somebody's name.

"Here is My servant," says God. "Here is somebody who does whatever I tell him to do—somebody I am delighted with—somebody I have specifically chosen and completely support. I have placed My Holy Spirit on him."

It begins to sound like one of those "Our speaker tonight is a fellow who needs no introduction," sort of things people say when they introduce somebody—except that, in all God is telling you about this person, God isn't telling you who it is.

"Here is…My servant."

So you know who this is in terms of his relationship with God. And certainly, relationship tells you a lot. "Let me introduce my spouse or my child, my friend or my coworker." That tells you a lot.

And God tells you even more about this servant of His by telling you what he's going to do with God's help. This servant is going to bring justice to the nations and establish that justice on earth. No small task. And if he can do that in a way that satisfies God, he is somebody worth knowing.

God tells you more still about this servant of His by telling you what the servant won't do.

He won't raise a ruckus—he won't be taking to the streets with a bull horn. This servant of God won't lift his hand to do damage even to fragile things. But he's going to change the world in a dramatic way, whoever he is.

He won't get it wrong or give up on his divine assignment before he gets it done—this "global justice thing" God has given him—directed him—to do. No wonder God is delighted with this guy—this chosen servant of God.

Maybe God doesn't tell you the servant's name because, all of a sudden, God remembers a few things He wants to tell the servant. Turning to the servant, God tells him,

> *"I have called you in righteousness;*
> *I will take hold of your hand.*
> *I will keep you*
>   *and make you a covenant...*
>   *and a light....*
> *Your job will be to open blind eyes*
>   *and set captives free*
>   *from dungeons and darkness."*

ॐज

Sounds like a pretty tall order, even for a personally selected servant of God: "Establish justice everywhere, without raising your voice in anger or raising your hand in violence. Don't get frustrated when things aren't going right in a world where everything always seems to go wrong. Don't let roadblocks block your way. Go ahead—do what I've told you to do—but not in your own power or cleverness. You be the vessel—the conduit—and I'll supply everything else necessary for the successful accomplishment of your mission."

God has introduced you to somebody and now you know how he relates to God, what God has given him to do, and how he will and won't go about doing it. But you still don't know who he is.

☜❖☞

Have you ever been to a carnival or county fair where they have these big, colorful pictures of people doing amazing things, except the faces are missing?

"Here is My servant," says God, but the face—the identity—is missing from the picture.

And it's not just one picture. Isaiah painted four of these pictures of this servant of God. Scholars call them "Servant Songs." Isaiah has painted these pictures and dropped them into his prophecies between chapters 42 and 53.[83] This is the first one.

These pictures were painted—these introductions from God of a chosen servant were written down—in the darkest days of Israel's history, after the destruction of the nation and many long years of captivity. God gives Isaiah the Prophet the vision to see that God has chosen someone to do something remarkable and wonderful. God has chosen someone to come and change the world in a way that no one ever had or ever could before.

In the other pictures, the servant is called to his task from the womb[84] and hidden by God until he is ready to perform it. Though the servant does not use violence to achieve his task, he is the target of violence from those who oppose him.[85] In fact, he becomes "a man of sorrows, acquainted with grief."[86] He will be pierced and

---

[83] Isaiah 42:1-4; 49:1-6; 50:4-11; 52:13—53:12.
[84] Isaiah 49:1, 5.
[85] Isaiah 50:6.
[86] Isaiah 53:3.

crushed, wounded because people think he deserves it.[87] And yet, because he doesn't, what he goes through will heal everyone, even those who do him the greatest harm.[88]

And while you hold that picture in your mind, see this as well: all of this suffering is part of God's plan and purpose for His chosen servant. It was the Lord's will to cause this servant to suffer, and after that, to see the light of life.[89]

But here's a question for you to ponder: Did God tell Isaiah who this person was or would be? If He did, Isaiah isn't telling, here or anywhere else in the book. Isaiah knew of servants of God in the past: Noah and Abraham and Moses and David. But none of their faces fit this picture. Even the prophet Jeremiah—who bears a passing resemblance—doesn't really provide the missing piece.

And there doesn't seem to be anybody else on Isaiah's horizon who even comes close.

But don't be surprised; that's the way divine revelation works: Everything you know about God comes to you through His gracious revelation, but even God's revelation does not reveal to you everything there is to know about God and His workings. There will always be mysteries remaining. God reveals to you only what He wants you to know—when He wants you to know it.[90]

So even as Isaiah is writing these Servant Songs under the inspiration of the Holy Spirit, he himself may be thinking, "I wonder who this servant is"—which is kind of funny in a spooky sort of way because that's exactly what the Ethiopian ambassador is asking himself and the early Christian disciple Philip when Philip turns up in the Gaza desert to meet him, six hundred years later, in Acts, Chapter 8.[91]

---

[87] Isaiah 53:4-5.
[88] Isaiah 53:6, 12.
[89] Isaiah 52:13; 53:10, 12.
[90] Deuteronomy 29:29.
[91] Acts 8:26-38.

"Who is the prophet talking about?" the African asks.

ঌ৵

And Philip knows the answer. Philip knows the name of the Servant of God because Philip met the Servant and saw Him do what God said in Isaiah His Servant would do. Philip began with that very passage in Isaiah 53 I mentioned earlier—one of the Servant Songs—and told the man he met in the desert the good news about Jesus.

Jesus, it turns out, was the Servant God chose to bring His divine justice to the earth.

"Here is God's Servant, my friend. And His name is Jesus—Jesus of Nazareth."

Jesus is the One God chose—long before His birth in Bethlehem—long before God inspired Isaiah to record the introduction. Jesus is the One God chose to uphold and inspire and empower. Jesus is the Servant God chose for changing the world.

Finally, a face to go with the pictures!

And so it gives me great pleasure this morning to introduce to you: Jesus Christ, the Servant of God, chosen before the foundation of the world,[92] upheld by God's "righteous, omnipotent Hand,"[93] the only-begotten Son of God in Whom God delights[94]—and was delighted to have all His divine fullness dwell,[95] so that He, Jesus, would bring God's justice to the earth,[96] reconciling all things,[97] including you, to God through His blood shed on the Cross.[98] Ladies and gentlemen—I give you: the Servant of God, Jesus Christ!

---

[92] 1 Peter 1:20.
[93] See Stanza 3, "How Firm a Foundation," authorship uncertain, 1787.
[94] Matthew 3:17.
[95] Colossians 1:19.
[96] Jeremiah 23:5.
[97] 2 Corinthians 5:18-19.
[98] Colossians 1:20.

101

Isaiah painted the pictures and the disciples saw Jesus and knew it was His face that fit perfectly in the faceless pictures they had been looking at all their lives.

And He does. Jesus is the perfect fit—the Servant of God, *par excellence.*

ॐ॰ॐ

But funny thing about those pictures without the faces: Anybody can step up and look through the opening. You can put your face there. I gathered a group together last Wednesday to help me work on this sermon—to talk about what Isaiah meant. Actually, it was the Wednesday night Youth Group, but I learned a lot as we discussed the passage.

When I asked them who they thought the servant of God was, one young lady didn't give me the answer I was expecting—the answer I have given you. She said, "Everybody." And I think she may be on to something.

If you believe that Jesus is the Servant of God and trust Him to do what God has given Him to do, you will become like Jesus in humility and obedience.[99] You will start to sense God upholding you[100] and putting His Spirit on you.[101] You will enjoy the delight God takes in you[102] and respond by approaching life as Jesus did, boldly and sacrificially.[103]

And as you submit yourself to God as Jesus did, and serve God as Jesus did, you start to look like Jesus,[104] like a chosen servant of God, helping Jesus complete the work of reconciling the world to God's will and way that God chose Jesus to perform.[105] Your face in the servant pictures may not look like quite the perfect fit that

---

[99] Philippians 2:8.
[100] Psalm 37:17.
[101] Acts 2:17-18.
[102] Matthew 25:21.
[103] 2 Corinthians 3:12; Romans 12:1.
[104] 1 Corinthians 15:49.
[105] 2 Corinthians 5:20.

the face of Jesus does, but it will look right enough as you let Jesus transform you into His image.[106]

God introduced His chosen servant, and Isaiah looked into the future for someone he did not know. The Church read Isaiah and saw Jesus on the Cross and knew they were looking at God's Servant. And you who have looked to Jesus and seen God's Servant in Him may now need to look in the mirror.

Where is God's servant whom He upholds—His chosen one in Whom He delights? Oh, risen from the dead[107] and sitting at the right hand of God the Father Almighty[108] from whence He shall come to judge the quick and the dead[109]—certainly—but also here in the house of God, sitting alongside other servants, worshipping the Father and growing in the image of His Son and serving God as He has chosen you and equipped you with His Spirit to do.

Remember what God says to His servant?

"I have called you in righteousness.
I will take hold of your hand.
I will keep you and make you a covenant
and a light to open eyes and set people free."

Well, if it's your face in the picture and your name He's calling, I guess you better get to work—like the servant of God you are.

ఌఄఞ

---

[106] Romans 8:29.
[107] 2 Timothy 2:8.
[108] Hebrews 10:12.
[109] 2 Timothy 4:1, KJV.

Isaiah 55:6-9 NRSV

⁶ Seek the LORD *while he may be found,*
call upon him while he is near;
⁷ let the wicked forsake their way,
and the unrighteous their thoughts;
let them return to the LORD*,*
that he may have mercy on them,
and to our God,
for he will abundantly pardon.
⁸ For my thoughts are not your thoughts,
nor are your ways my ways, says the LORD*.*
⁹ For as the heavens are higher than the earth,
so are my ways higher than your ways
and my thoughts than your thoughts.

ঙ৽৵

14.

Lost and Found

Isaiah 55:6-9 NRSV

A week or so ago, I lost my sunglasses. I didn't worry about it—the first day or so. I'm absent-minded. I misplace things. I figured they would turn up.

They didn't.

After a few days, I was bothered enough to start looking for them seriously. I looked in all the places around the house I usually drop them. I went through all the pockets of the pants and coats I had worn recently. Then, I went through the pockets of all my clothes. I looked in drawers and out in the cars.

They don't seem to be in my house or the cars or the office here. I don't know where they are, and I don't think I'm going to find them, wherever they are.

I probably dropped them somewhere. I should have taken better care of them. I should have paid more attention to them. I had gotten to where I didn't think much about them. Now, I realize how much I need them. But where are they? I don't know.

&-§

The children of Israel had lost more than sunglasses. They had lost their struggle against the invading Babylonian army. They had lost their country, Judah, and their capital, Jerusalem. They had lost their Davidic king and their holy Temple. They had lost their prosperity and their freedom and, many of them, their lives. Those who were left—who were taken into exile—lost their homes and their hope and, many of them, their God.

Actually, they had lost their God long before they were conquered and hauled off to Babylon. Their relationship with God had gotten old, and they got to where they didn't think much about it. They should have paid more attention to it and taken better care of it.

They didn't worry about their relationship with God until they needed God. When things got bad, they figured God would turn up. But He didn't. Where was God? They didn't know.

৯৽৵

And then, decades after the dust from the disaster I just mentioned had settled—a lifetime after the Jewish survivors had settled into their second-class citizenship in Babylon—with the glamorous gods of their conquerors crowding them on every side, a guy shows up telling them: "Seek the Lord—seek *your* God— while He may be found. *Call* upon Him—the God you had long ago given up on—while He is near."

In fact, this guy tells the Jews—the children of Israel—the people of God—to do four things: seek, call, forsake, return. And we'll come back to that.

But, for now, notice *why* he tells them to do these things.

"The God you lost and gave up ever finding *can* be found. This God is near. And this God—*your* God—will have mercy on you and abundantly pardon you for everything you've done wrong— everything you did or did not do in your relationship with Him that caused you to lose track of Him."

৯৽৵

We live among a people—we may be a people—who live as though we have lost our God. We've taken Him for granted so long that many have simply and completely misplaced Him. "Don't worry," we think, "He'll turn up when we need Him."

But what if He doesn't. We think times are hard now. What if they get a lot worse? Will we find God then? Will He even allow us to? Where will God be then?

I've lost some things that I have never found. They are gone forever. I've lost other things and found them again. What a great experience!

If you've lost your God, the guidance is clear: Seek Him *now*—while He may be found. Call upon Him *now*—while He is near enough to hear you and graciously disposed to listen. Forsake whatever it is that distracts you from your relationship with God and displeases Him. Turn your back on turning your back on God. And return to this God—your God—Who can and will have mercy on you and pardon you, in full, from your spiritual absent-mindedness and moral inattention.

The day will come for each of us when you realize how much you need God. When that day comes, it will be far better to have found God and returned to Him already than to need Him and not know where to look—to call out to Him and hear no answer.

Today, seek the Lord and call upon Him. Return to Him and receive His pardon. Find the God you've lost.

ॐ◌ॐ

From the Book of Jeremiah

Jeremiah 1:1-10 ESV

¹ The words of Jeremiah, the son of Hilkiah, one of the priests who were in Anathoth in the land of Benjamin, ² to whom the word of the LORD *came in the days of Josiah the son of Amon, king of Judah, in the thirteenth year of his reign. ³ It came also in the days of Jehoiakim the son of Josiah, king of Judah, and until the end of the eleventh year of Zedekiah, the son of Josiah, king of Judah, until the captivity of Jerusalem in the fifth month.*

⁴ Now the word of the LORD *came to me, saying,*

> *⁵ "Before I formed you in the womb I knew you,*
> *and before you were born I consecrated you;*
> *I appointed you a prophet to the nations."*

⁶ Then I said, "Ah, Lord GOD*! Behold, I do not know how to speak, for I am only a youth."*

⁷ But the LORD *said to me,*

> *"Do not say, 'I am only a youth';*
> *for to all to whom I send you,*
> *you shall go,*
> *and whatever I command you,*
> *you shall speak.*
> *⁸ Do not be afraid of them,*
> *for I am with you to deliver you,*
> *declares the* LORD*."*

⁹ Then the LORD *put out his hand and touched my mouth. And the* LORD *said to me,*

> *"Behold, I have put my words in your mouth.*
> *¹⁰ See, I have set you this day*
> *over nations and over kingdoms,*
> *to pluck up and to break down,*
> *to destroy and to overthrow,*
> *to build and to plant."*

John 15:16-19, 26-27 ESV

[Jesus said:]

^{16} *"You did not choose me, but I chose you and appointed you that you should go and bear fruit and that your fruit should abide, so that whatever you ask the Father in my name, he may give it to you.* ^{17} *These things I command you, so that you will love one another.*

^{18} *"If the world hates you, know that it has hated me before it hated you.* ^{19} *If you were of the world, the world would love you as its own; but because you are not of the world, but I chose you out of the world, therefore the world hates you.*

^{26} *"But when the Helper comes, whom I will send to you from the Father, the Spirit of truth, who proceeds from the Father, he will bear witness about me.* ^{27} *And you also will bear witness, because you have been with me from the beginning."*

శ్రీ

15.

Since Before You Were Born

Jeremiah 1:1-10; John 15:16-19, 26-27 ESV

Just outside that door, we are taking pictures of our members for our church directory—another great reason to become a member of Trinity, by the way. The purpose for taking the pictures is to help you get to know everybody, and to help everybody get to know you.

This picture will probably not be the first picture ever taken of you. You may have pictures of yourself all the way back to when you were born. Now, with ultra-sound technology, we're taking pictures of people *before* they are born. Isn't it remarkable that you can see and know a person before he or she has even left the womb? Remarkable for us, perhaps—but God has been doing it since the dawn of time. Listen again to what God said to Jeremiah:

> *"Before I formed you in the womb I knew you,*
> *and before you were born I consecrated you;*
> *I appointed you…"*

(apparently, before Jeremiah was born and perhaps even before his conception in his mother's womb)

> *"…a prophet to the nations."*

❧

I want to unpack what God says here, but before I do, you need to know that, in this regard, Jeremiah is not a special case. The Psalmist acknowledged of God,

> *"...You created my inmost being;*
> *You knit me together in my mother's womb."*[110]

Job, speaking of himself and his servants, said,

> *"Did not he—*
> *who made me in the womb—*
> *make them?"*[111]

And in addressing all the Jewish people, the prophet Isaiah began a prophecy with these words,

> *"This is what the LORD says—*
> *he who made you,*
> *who formed you in the womb..."*[112]

God says—to every one of us—

> *"before I formed you in the womb, I knew you."*

◈◈◈

Two things: God *"formed you in the womb,"* and even before that, He *"knew you."*

Do you hear what the Bible is saying about *you?* God formed you in your mother's womb. Now, the Bible is not a primitive *Grey's Anatomy*[113]—it is not a medical textbook. They didn't know, back then, all the technical terms or much about the scientific specifics of human reproduction. That's not the point. God *formed* you.

God not only decided what you would be and who you would be, He caused the coming together of all the stuff that caused you

---

[110] Psalm 139:13, NIV.

[111] Job 31:15, NIV.

[112] Isaiah 44:2, NIV.

[113] *Grey's Anatomy*, 41st Edition, Susan Standring, ed., Amsterdam, Netherlands: Elsevier, 2015. The 1st Edition, published in London in 1858, was written by Henry Gray and illustrated by Henry Vandyke Carter.

to be at all and caused you to be the absolutely unique individual you are—minus what you and this sinful world have done with His handiwork since. Now, we know so much more about the biology and the chemistry and genetics involved, but we appreciate so much less the divine miracle of the thing. God formed all of us— every one of us—and, therefore, *you.*

Listen again to what the Psalmist said:

> *"You created my inmost being;*
> *You knit me together..."*

Those two verbs are not accidental. God *created* your inmost being. The Power that caused the entire universe to come into being out of nothing, by the mere expression of His will, called forth into existence your inmost being—your immortal soul— your eternal spirit—just by wanting it to be so.

And then God knit you together. Some of you are knitters. Some of you knit as a ministry in this church. Knitting is a very personal—very intimate—activity. It is hands-on. It requires skill, patience and commitment to ensure every movement of the fingers connects the parts correctly according to the pattern. When God does it, it is a gentle way of bringing a beautiful and intricate body together around a sacred soul. And so it was with you. The Creator of all the universe spoke your soul and spirit into existence and then spent nine-months carefully knitting you together in your mother's womb. That is who you are. That's the picture you need to see. The Psalmist ponders that and exclaims,

> *"I am fearfully and wonderfully made!"*[114]

❧

But even before that, the Bible says, God knew you.

I said earlier that we're taking pictures for our directory so you can get to know each other. But in reality, the pictures are only going to help you put a face to a name. There's a lot more to

---

[114] Psalm 139:14, NIV.

knowing someone. It's kind of like what our architects will be doing for us. First, they will provide conceptual drawings. They will show us what the buildings will look like. When we approve the concept, they will get to work on construction documents—the blueprints that show how every detail will fit together inside and out to make this facility exactly what it is supposed to be. A talented builder will be able to look at those documents and "see" the finished product—he will know our church intimately before he does the first thing to build it.

God conceived you and drew up the blueprints for you in His mind even before He created your soul and began to form your body. God knew what you were supposed to be, and how you would be equipped to fulfill His purpose for designing you, before He ever reached into your mother's womb to begin the knitting together of your being—your life. And when they refer to "the miracle of human life"—they don't know the half of it.

But God does. God knows everything there is to know about you—and always has. God knows *about* you in full and complete detail—He designed the plan and constructed you in faithful compliance with it. And He *knows* you. God knows who you have become and why you have become who you are. He knows who you could be and should be. He knows who you will be, based on whatever choices you will make as you go forward in your life. The God Who knew you completely when you were only the knowledge of His plan for you in His mind, knows you now and will always know you, throughout all eternity (wherever you choose to spend it).

❧

But there is more: *"Before you were born, I set you apart."*

At least, that's the modern, English translation. Before we became theologically illiterate, the word was "consecrate." It carries a lot more weight than just "set apart." God designed you before He ever formed you for a specific, divinely determined and desired purpose and function. God meant for you to be. And as God was knitting your body together around your soul, God said, "This one will be for Me. This person is for My work and will be able to do holy things for Me."

That's what you are for. That's the reason for your life.

"I have made you in such a way that you will be able to do and be appropriate for the special, holy things I want to do with you."

There was an old quiz show that used to air on TV years ago— a show in which panelists would be given unusual looking objects and asked to explain their purpose.[115] The panelists didn't know what any of these things were for, and so they made something up. That's what we do with our lives. When you don't know that you were made to be a sacred, consecrated instrument for the service of God, you make something up. The TV explanations were usually silly. In real life, not knowing you have been consecrated can be tragic.

To be consecrated is not just to be set apart, but to be set apart for what is good, and kept away from what is evil. It is to be devoted so completely to the holy things of God that the holy God will dwell with you and work through you and be happy with you.

You were consecrated since before you were born—by the very God Who made you. Consecrated and appointed.

Jeremiah was appointed by God to be a prophet to the nations. The Lord appointed Moses to lead the children of Israel out of Egypt,[116] and David, later, to rule over them.[117] Jesus appointed disciples, first 12[118] and then 70,[119] and then all of us.[120] Whenever it was you recognized that God had appointed you to a divine task, the appointment was actually made before you were born. Since

---

[115] *The Liar's Club*, 1969-1970, 1976-1979.
[116] Exodus 3:10.
[117] 1 Samuel 16:1-6.
[118] Mark 3:13-14.
[119] Luke 10:1.
[120] Matthew 28:19-20.

before you were born, God knew the plan He had for you, the sacred purpose for which He formed you.

God formed you and knew you and consecrated you and appointed you. Feeling intimidated? So were Jeremiah and Isaiah[121] and Moses[122] and everybody else who had any sense. A thousand excuses come to mind to beg off the divine appointment. God has heard them all.

Jeremiah said, "I don't know how," which sounds suspiciously like "I don't want to," since God can provide all the knowledge and ability to do whatever He appoints you to do. And if you wanted to, you would pray for what you need to do the job, and God would give it.[123]

Jeremiah's other excuse was "I am only a child," which is just another way of saying, "I can't." That "I am only..." excuse can be filled in with a lot of blanks:

"I am only a child."

"I am only an old person."

"I am only a layman."

"I am only a housewife."

"I am only a new Christian."

"I am only a duffer...."[124]

Well, anyway—the idea that God formed and fashioned you for His will, and gave you life to get on with the work for which you were consecrated and appointed, calls to mind every possible reason for exemption. But God just won't hear it. "Don't say, 'I am only *anything*,'" says God. "You are everything I want and need you to be. I made sure of that, long ago"

"And don't be afraid. I formed you—I knew you—I consecrated you—I appointed you—all before you were born. Now I send you—I command you—and I will be with you."

---

[121] Isaiah 6:5.

[122] Exodus 3:11.

[123] James 1:5-6.

[124] This sermon was preached in a church located in an avid golfing community.

"I have put My words in your mouth and I have set you over nations to pluck up and tear down, to undermine and to overthrow, to build and to plant."

"Wait a minute, Preacher; that's *Jeremiah's* call!"

And yours.

"You have not chosen Me," says the Son of God, *"but I have chosen you and appointed you that you should go and bear fruit."*

"But I don't know how!"

"Whatever you ask the Father in My Name, He will give you."

"But I'm only…!"

"You will receive power when the Holy Spirit comes on you and you will be My witnesses…"[125]

"Do not worry…about what to say. Just say whatever is given you at the time, for it is not you speaking, but the Holy Spirit."[126]

"And, lo, I am with you always.…"[127]

God has created you and called you to be a part of His breaking down of this sinful world and the rebuilding of lives according to His spiritual blueprints. This is who you are. This is what He wants. God knows you can do it.

Now you know it, too.

❧

---

[125] Acts 1:8, NIV.
[126] Mark 13:11, NIV.
[127] Matthew 28:20, KJV.

.

Jeremiah 17:5-8 ESV

⁵ *Thus says the* L*ORD:*

"Cursed is the man who trusts in man
and makes flesh his strength,
whose heart turns away from the L*ORD.*
⁶ *He is like a shrub in the desert,*
and shall not see any good come.
He shall dwell
in the parched places of the wilderness,
in an uninhabited salt land.

⁷ *"Blessed is the man who trusts in the* L*ORD,*
whose trust is the L*ORD.*
⁸ *He is like a tree planted by water,*
that sends out its roots by the stream,
and does not fear when heat comes,
for its leaves remain green,
and is not anxious in the year of drought,
for it does not cease to bear fruit."

৵৽

Romans 8:1-11 ESV

[1] *There is therefore now no condemnation for those who are in Christ Jesus.* [2] *For the law of the Spirit of life has set you free in Christ Jesus from the law of sin and death.* [3] *For God has done what the law, weakened by the flesh, could not do. By sending his own Son in the likeness of sinful flesh and for sin he condemned sin in the flesh,* [4] *in order that the righteous requirement of the law might be fulfilled in us, who walk not according to the flesh but according to the Spirit.* [5] *For those who live according to the flesh set their minds on the things of the flesh, but those who live according to the Spirit set their minds on the things of the Spirit.* [6] *For to set the mind on the flesh is death, but to set the mind on the Spirit is life and peace.* [7] *For the mind that is set on the flesh is hostile to God, for it does not submit to God's law; indeed, it cannot.* [8] *Those who are in the flesh cannot please God.*

[9] *You, however, are not in the flesh but in the Spirit, if in fact the Spirit of God dwells in you. Anyone who does not have the Spirit of Christ does not belong to him.* [10] *But if Christ is in you, although the body is dead because of sin, the Spirit is life because of righteousness.* [11] *If the Spirit of him who raised Jesus from the dead dwells in you, he who raised Christ Jesus from the dead will also give life to your mortal bodies through his Spirit who dwells in you.*

তে•ও

16.

One Way or the Other

Jeremiah 17:5-8; Romans 8:1-11 ESV

Everybody—every day—has to answer the same bedeviling question: "Which way?"

In everything we do or say, we're confronted with an option: "Which way?"

Even when there seems to be only one way—or no way—the question really won't go away: "Is this the right way—the best way—the only way?"

The truth is that even when there seem to be many ways—to live your life—to raise your family—to order your society—to strengthen your church—to sustain your nation—to secure your eternity—there are really only two. And, of those, only one actually works. Only one way works.

The two ways—and here I would say, "of life"—except that only the one way that works is actually "of—life." The other "way of life" is not a way of life at all; it's a way of death.

But more about that in a minute….

The "two ways" have gone by different names throughout history. Today, we often call them "the secular" and "the sacred."

There is the person who believes reality is limited to what may be labeled "the natural order."

And there is the person who senses—and therefore submits and opens himself to—an additional and greater reality beyond what man can comprehend and control.

The Prophet Jeremiah called the two ways "trusting in man" and "trusting in the Lord." The Apostle Paul called them "living according to the flesh" and "living according to the Spirit."

And these are—always—the only two options you really have in life.

All the options that seem to be out there—all the nuances and variations and distinctions you may think you have chosen—they all boil down, in the end, to "with God" or "without God"—under God's authority, control and empowerment—or not.

And Jeremiah says that God says that the secularist—however distinct or diverse his variation—is cursed. Blessing is only available to the person who commits himself to the sacred—who trusts in God so completely that God actually *is* his trust. And not just any God. We're talking about the God Who spoke through Jeremiah—and Paul—and in a unique way through Someone else I'll mention in a minute.

It seems rather harsh to say that people who choose to live secular lives are cursed. There are an awful lot of them—more and more all the time. And a lot of these people are our relatives and our friends. At one time—and perhaps not too long ago for some of us—they were us. But—hard as it seems—this is what the Bible says.

᠃᠂᠂

Now, having said that, I need to quibble with the translation we use in the 9:00 service—the "NewSong" service—on one point. The *Good News Translation* renders the original Hebrew in verse 5 of Jeremiah 17 this way: *"The Lord says, 'I will condemn those who…put their trust in human beings….'"*

It sounds like a threat—a promise of punishment: "I [God] will [actively] condemn!" The translation we use in the other two services—the *English Standard Version*—just has God stating a fact without taking any action: "those who put their trust…in human beings *are cursed*." And that's a better translation.

God doesn't have to do anything to those who have chosen to live without Him—or those who have tried to get Him to live with them on their own terms—for them to be cursed. They have cursed their own lives, themselves—without any help from God—because, as Jeremiah pictures it, they have "planted" themselves in a place that provides nothing to keep them nourished and alive.

Here's what you've got to understand: the "way" itself is cursed. This is not God issuing a threat. It's just God stating a universal and unalterable fact: the way of life without God—in whatever form it takes—is, by its very nature, a godless way that leads to death rather than life—no matter how good or nice or important the person is who chooses it. The godless way is barren, for all its seeming beauty. It is dry as death, for all its apparent appeal.

The man who trusts in man—in the ultimate sense—is cursed, and it doesn't matter if the "man" you trust in is you yourself, someone in your family, your military comrades, your social circle, popular celebrities, your political party, your church or your country. Yes, we depend on others for many things, from trivial stuff to matters of great importance. And we seek to be dependable ourselves in fulfilling our obligations to others. And all that is well and good as far as it goes.

But when we do not put our trust in God—when we do not live according to the Spirit of God—everything we do or hope others will do for us is finally a bust because we remain cursed. It is God alone Who can give life, and God only gives life to those who have chosen to trust in Him and live according to the Spirit. And if God doesn't do what we need to have done, we're doomed.

But so many ways look so good. The Proverbs say in more than one place: *"There is a way which seems right to a man, but its end is the way to death."*[128] That's the way that is other than God's way. That's the bad news—and it's truly awful.

But here's the good news: *"There is now no condemnation for those who are in Christ Jesus. For the law of the Spirit of life in Christ Jesus has set me free from the law of sin and death."*

There *is* another way, other than the way that is cursed. *"Blessed is the man who trusts in the LORD."* And let's be clear: we're not talking about "being spiritual" or "supporting the idea of religion" or "trying to be a good person." Paul means those who walk according to the Spirit and not the flesh—those whose minds are set on the Spirit and not on the things of the flesh. Jeremiah says the man who trusts in the Lord so completely and thoroughly that the Lord *is* his trust is blessed—like a tree that is going to flourish however hard the hardships get because his roots will get down deep in the kind of soil that never dries up no matter what the bad weather brings.

"There is a way that leads to life"—but only *one* way: total trust in God—Who has blessed our trust by bringing His Son Jesus Christ into our world—and Who blesses our lives even now by bringing His Son Jesus Christ into them.

❧

So, which way? Sacred or secular? Trusting God or trusting man? With God—on His terms—or without Him on any terms? According to the Spirit or according to the flesh? Blessed or cursed? Life or death?

It's one way—or the other.

❧

---

[128] Proverbs 14:12; 16:25, RSV.

From the Book of Lamentations

Lamentations 3:19-26 ESV

¹⁹ *Remember my affliction and my wanderings,*
the wormwood and the gall!
²⁰ *My soul continually remembers it*
and is bowed down within me.
²¹ *But this I call to mind,*
and therefore I have hope:
²² *The steadfast love of the* LORD *never ceases;*
his mercies never come to an end;
²³ *they are new every morning;*
great is your faithfulness.
²⁴ *"The* LORD *is my portion," says my soul,*
"therefore I will hope in him."
²⁵ *The* LORD *is good to those who wait for him,*
to the soul who seeks him.
²⁶ *It is good that one should wait quietly*
for the salvation of the LORD.

❧❧

John 16:2-22, 33 ESV

[Jesus said:]

²"They will put you out of the synagogues. Indeed, the hour is coming when whoever kills you will think he is offering service to God. ³ And they will do these things because they have not known the Father, nor me. ⁴ But I have said these things to you, that when their hour comes you may remember that I told them to you. I did not say these things to you from the beginning, because I was with you. ⁵ But now I am going to him who sent me, and none of you asks me, 'Where are you going?' ⁶ But because I have said these things to you, sorrow has filled your heart. ⁷ Nevertheless, I tell you the truth: it is to your advantage that I go away, for if I do not go away, the Helper will not come to you. But if I go, I will send him to you. ⁸ And when he comes, he will convict the world concerning sin and righteousness and judgment: ⁹ concerning sin, because they do not believe in me; ¹⁰ concerning righteousness, because I go to the Father, and you will see me no longer; ¹¹ concerning judgment, because the ruler of this world is judged.

¹² "I still have many things to say to you, but you cannot bear them now. ¹³ When the Spirit of truth comes, he will guide you into all the truth, for he will not speak on his own authority, but whatever he hears he will speak, and he will declare to you the things that are to come. ¹⁴ He will glorify me, for he will take what is mine and declare it to you. ¹⁵ All that the Father has is mine; therefore I said that he will take what is mine and declare it to you.

¹⁶ "A little while, and you will see me no longer; and again a little while, and you will see me." ¹⁷ So some of his disciples said to one another, "What is this that he says to us, 'A little while, and you will not see me, and again a little while, and you will see me'; and, 'because I am going to the Father'?" ¹⁸ So they were saying, "What does he mean by 'a little while'? We do not know what he is talking about." ¹⁹ Jesus knew that they wanted to ask him, so he said to them, "Is this what you are asking yourselves, what I meant by saying, 'A little while and you will not see me, and again a little while and you will see me'? ²⁰ Truly, truly, I say to you, you will weep and lament, but the world will rejoice. You will be sorrowful, but your sorrow will turn into joy.

²¹ *When a woman is giving birth, she has sorrow because her hour has come, but when she has delivered the baby, she no longer remembers the anguish, for joy that a human being has been born into the world.*

²² *"So also you have sorrow now, but I will see you again, and your hearts will rejoice, and no one will take your joy from you."*

³³ *"I have said these things to you, that in me you may have peace. In the world you will have tribulation. But take heart; I have overcome the world."*

୬∘୬

17.

Remembering This and That

Lamentations 3:19-26; John 16:2-22, 33 ESV

"How lonely sits the city that was full of people!
How like a widow has she become...
She who was a princess...
*   has become a slave.*
She weeps bitterly in the night...."[129]

৵৽৶

So begins the Book of Lamentations, an attempt on the part of
God's people to make sense of the destruction of Jerusalem, their
capital city, and their exile from it. The devastation was complete.
The suffering and loss were unbearable. And it was worse for those
who did not die than for those who did, because for the survivors,
as for the city itself, the agony and sense of helplessness just went
on without end. What can you do—what can you say—when your
world goes up in smoke?

৵৽৶

---

[129] Lamentations 1:1-2, ESV.

We don't go to Lamentations very often—it's too depressing. You'll probably go a very long time before you hear another sermon from any text in this book.

So why spend a Sunday here now?

I think the reason relates to our growing sense that things are not right in our society—among our people—that our country is becoming something God will not indefinitely permit.

Those of us who have been around for a while—long enough to have seen the broader trend of history—are depressed—and, frankly, frightened—by what we see. Things we could not have imagined are now commonplace. The moral and the immoral have traded places in public perception—and popular practice. And if the age-old Word of God has any ongoing relevance—which more and more people deny—but if the Bible remains God's active and authoritative Word for modern humanity, we run the same risk as the people the Bible first addressed did.

There is an old song that goes,

> "Dreams can come true,
> it can happen to you,
> if you're young at heart."[130]

It may also be that

> "*Prophesies* can come true,
> it can happen to you,
> if you're *hard of* heart."

The people of Jerusalem could not imagine that their capital could be destroyed—their land overrun—their way of life wiped out.

And then, the impossible happened.

"Yes, but Judah was a dinky little kingdom! She was surrounded by a bunch of big empires. Of course, *she* could be conquered."

---

[130] Johnny Richards and Carolyn Leigh, "Young at Heart," 1953.

132

But remember, the great empires that conquered the petty kingdoms were also, in their turns, conquered. Even the mighty fall. Assyria and Egypt, Babylon and Persia, and later, Rome itself– all overrun as easily as Judah and Jerusalem had been in the end. It is God Who raises up nations and brings them down, not their governments or their armies or their people.

So what do you do if the unimaginable happens and the world as you know it comes to an end?

The Book of Lamentations is the guidebook for getting through the greatest catastrophes you can go through. Death and destruction, tragedy and trauma, grief and pain, fear and despair— it's all there in Lamentations, without any sugar coating, short cuts or snake oil con jobs. And the secret is in "remembering."

෬෨

A line from another old song:
> "Memories may be beautiful and yet,
> what's too painful to remember,
> we simply chose to forget."[131]

It's a lovely sentiment, but it's not true. Really painful things are too painful to *forget*.

You remember them even when you want to forget them. When you try to forget them, the pain gets worse. When you try to avoid them or ignore them, they find a way to come back into your consciousness bigger and "badder" than ever.

And so, in the first two chapters of Lamentations, Jerusalem is personified—the city is presented—as an abandoned, grieving, destitute woman, whose protective and providing husband the king has been killed and whose children have all been taken from her. And she remembers everything that she has suffered—and continues to suffer—with no sense that the suffering will ever end.

---

[131] Alan Bergman, Marilyn Bergman and Marvin Hamlisch, "The Way We Were," theme song from the 1974 movie of the same name.

"You've got to walk this lonesome valley.
You've got to walk it by yourself.
O, nobody else can walk it for you.
You've got to walk it by yourself."[132]

And that's just what "Lady" Jerusalem does. She cannot avoid what has happened, or make it go away, and so she endures it and grieves it to the full. When the sky falls in on you, you can't escape it—but you don't have to like it. You can call it what it is. And you don't have to keep how you feel about it a secret. She—Jerusalem—remembers what she has gone through and cries out in her anguish.

And then, she remembers something else. She remembers *why* she is going through such horrors:

"The LORD is in the right,
for I have rebelled against his word..."[133]

she says.

And to God:

"...you have dealt with me
because of all my transgressions..."[134]

What happened to Jerusalem and her "children" was her fault—their fault. They had been warned—for centuries—by all kinds of prophets. But the people had not listened. And now—when all their chickens finally came home to roost—there was, seemingly, nobody to listen to her.

But to remember *why* you're in the fix you're in—and to acknowledge it—to repent of what you did wrong, even when it's too late to prevent the terrible judgment that resulted from doing the wrong in the first place—this is an important and essential step in getting through the grief that engulfs you.

She has acknowledged her guilt to anyone who would listen—including God—and the writer who has been describing what's

---

132 "Jesus Walked This Lonesome Valley," American folk hymn.
133 Lamentations 1:18, ESV.
134 Lamentations 1:22, ESV.

going on tells her, "You're grieving; grieve to God. Your heart is broken; pour out what's in your heart to Him."[135]

When your world comes apart—and especially when it's your own fault—you may feel like you've got nowhere to go with your grief. Just goes to show: Your feelings don't always tell you the truth.

Jerusalem, like a defiled and destitute mother, remembers her pain and suffering and her responsibility for bringing the judgment on herself and her children. And in remembering this, she survives, when there seems no way she could.

৯৩

And then, in Chapter 3, somebody else appears: "a man of constant sorrow,"[136] if the first few verses are any indication:

"I am the man who has seen affliction
...again and again the whole day long."[137]

Somebody has it "in" for this man, whom we should probably understand as the personification of all those taken out of Jerusalem into exile. He is the Jewish exile "everyman."

Anyway, Someone has it in for him and that Someone turns out to be God.

Like "Lady" Jerusalem, the man remembers everything he has suffered in the course of the utter destruction of his world. He can't forget it and it crushes his soul inside him.

But crushed beneath the weight of the world, the man remembers something else, too.

He has forgotten what happiness is, but all at once, he remembers something that gives him hope—in spite of everything. He remembers this:

---

[135] Lamentations 2:18-19.
[136] "Man of Constant Sorrow," traditional American folk song, popularized by the movie, *O Brother, Where Art Thou,* 2000.
[137] Lamentations 3:1, 3, ESV.

> *"The steadfast love of the LORD never ceases;*
> *His mercies never come to an end;*
> *they are new every morning...."*

God is the One Who caused—or allowed—the catastrophe God's people suffered. They sinned against Him and they got what they deserved. And what they got seems like more than they can bear. This man who is suffering more than he can stand cannot remember the good times.

But in the darkest depths of despair, he remembers something more important—about God. God's love and God's mercy do not—will not—end. They will last longer than his suffering and his grief—than anyone's suffering and grief.

God's unconditional love and unmeasurable mercy will never end. But the man's suffering—Jerusalem's suffering—God's people's suffering—*your* suffering—will. And when the suffering God's people experience ends, God's love and mercy will be there, just as they have been there throughout the suffering.

Notice that the man's hope didn't come from how he *felt*, but from something he remembered—something he *couldn't* feel in the midst of his suffering. The man *knew* something about God, and he remembered it when he needed desperately to remember it. He remembered God's great faithfulness, which means that God's love and mercy are the same today as they were every day before, and as they will be for every day to come. It's like they're "new every morning." God's goodness does not run out of gas.

What else does the man remember?

He remembers that God is good to those who wait for Him and seek Him. Now this may sound contradictory: "wait and seek." One sounds passive and the other sounds active.

To "wait" is to be where God wants you to be—to stay where He puts you. To "wait" is to trust God to show up when you need Him to. To "wait" is to let God take the lead in what you do—and where you go—and when you go. To "wait" is to trust God to do what He says He will do.

136

To "seek"—even as you wait—is to desire to see God. It is to anticipate His coming to you—to be focused on noticing His presence at the earliest possible opportunity so that you are aware of His presence with you as soon and as much as possible.

Not "wait and see," which means "maybe so—maybe not." But wait and *seek*. Wait quietly, in complete confidence—even in your suffering—for the salvation of God. And know that He is there, bringing the salvation you need. And look for it, all the time.

❧

It is amazing that, in the midst of these anguished outpourings of grief and pain and seeming hopelessness, a beautiful word of hope would emerge. Heartache and trauma are hard soil for hope to grow in, but since I'm quoting old songs, let me share one more:
"When the night has been too lonely—
and the road has been too long...
Just remember: in the winter,
far beneath the bitter snow,
lies the seed that, with the sun's love—"
(or God's love—and mercy—)
"in the spring, becomes the rose—"
(the rose of God's healing and salvation that He has planted in you).[138]

❧

Lamentations—this little book so steeped in sorrow—is God's guide to hope in terrible darkness. You may use it for your personal needs—when you are suffering more than you think you can stand.

But the day may be coming when the need will no longer be personal or private—when we will all need to make sense of God's judgment on our rebellious world.

---

[138] Amanda McBroom, "The Rose," 1977.

And when that day comes, we will need to remember "this and that"—our guilt—and our hope…in God's steadfast love and unending mercy.

ॐॐ

From the Book of Ezekiel

Ezekiel 37:1-14 ESV

¹ *The hand of the* LORD *was upon me, and he brought me out in the Spirit of the* LORD *and set me down in the middle of the valley; it was full of bones.* ² *And he led me around among them, and behold, there were very many on the surface of the valley, and behold, they were very dry.* ³ *And he said to me, "Son of man, can these bones live?" And I answered, "O Lord* GOD, *you know."* ⁴ *Then he said to me, "Prophesy over these bones, and say to them, O dry bones, hear the word of the* LORD. ⁵ *Thus says the Lord* GOD *to these bones: Behold, I will cause breath to enter you, and you shall live.* ⁶ *And I will lay sinews upon you, and will cause flesh to come upon you, and cover you with skin, and put breath in you, and you shall live, and you shall know that I am the* LORD*."*

⁷ *So I prophesied as I was commanded. And as I prophesied, there was a sound, and behold, a rattling, and the bones came together, bone to its bone.* ⁸ *And I looked, and behold, there were sinews on them, and flesh had come upon them, and skin had covered them. But there was no breath in them.* ⁹ *Then he said to me, "Prophesy to the breath; prophesy, son of man, and say to the breath, Thus says the Lord* GOD: *Come from the four winds, O breath, and breathe on these slain, that they may live."* ¹⁰ *So I prophesied as he commanded me, and the breath came into them, and they lived and stood on their feet, an exceedingly great army.*

¹¹ *Then he said to me, "Son of man, these bones are the whole house of Israel. Behold, they say, 'Our bones are dried up, and our hope is lost; we are indeed cut off.'* ¹² *Therefore prophesy, and say to them, Thus says the* LORD GOD: *Behold, I will open your graves and raise you from your graves, O my people. And I will bring you into the land of Israel.* ¹³ *And you shall know that I am the* LORD, *when I open your graves, and raise you from your graves, O my people.* ¹⁴ *And I will put my Spirit within you, and you shall live, and I will place you in your own land. Then you shall know that I am the* LORD; *I have spoken, and I will do it, declares the* LORD*."*

❧❧

John 5:21-29 ESV

[Jesus said:]

²¹ *"For as the Father raises the dead and gives them life, so also the Son gives life to whom he will.* ²² *For the Father judges no one, but has given all judgment to the Son,* ²³ *that all may honor the Son, just as they honor the Father. Whoever does not honor the Son does not honor the Father who sent him.* ²⁴ *Truly, truly, I say to you, whoever hears my word and believes him who sent me has eternal life. He does not come into judgment, but has passed from death to life.*

²⁵ *"Truly, truly, I say to you, an hour is coming, and is now here, when the dead will hear the voice of the Son of God, and those who hear will live.* ²⁶ *For as the Father has life in himself, so he has granted the Son also to have life in himself.* ²⁷ *And he has given him authority to execute judgment, because he is the Son of Man.* ²⁸ *Do not marvel at this, for an hour is coming when all who are in the tombs will hear his voice* ²⁹ *and come out, those who have done good to the resurrection of life, and those who have done evil to the resurrection of judgment."*

੦ৼ৽

18.

When God Puts Your Life Back Together

Ezekiel 37:1-14; John 5:21-29 ESV

Early in the movie *Patton*[139]—after the opening scene with the giant flag, but before anything else—the general is taken out to a vast empty field.

He looks out across it, mesmerized, with the haunting sound of a bugle call echoing faintly in the background: "DA-da-da, DA-da-da, DA-da-da." It is the site of an ancient battle, he tells his companions. He describes the carnage that took place there as though he can see it vividly, even at that moment. And then he tells them, "I was there." The reaction of those around him is not hard to imagine.

The reaction was probably similar to that of the Jewish exiles in Babylon when the prophet Ezekiel told them about his experience in the Valley of the Dry Bones. Ezekiel had been important enough in Jerusalem to have been taken to Babylonian exile early, a decade before the final destruction of the city. In Exile, he and his companions, the former leaders of Judah's political and religious establishment, were helpless spectators as

[139] Movie *Patton*, music by Jerry Goldsmith, 1970.

their country was conquered, the last king deposed, and their sacred Temple destroyed.

Many of their friends and family members had died in the months of siege or been killed in the final, violent attacks. The survivors were bound and brought to Babylon to become the latest part of the Exile community. Only the poorest peasants had been left to eke out a pitiful existence in what was left of the Promised Land.

Everything they valued had been wiped away. The world—the life—they knew, was gone, seemingly forever. Psalm 137 captures the sense of corporate trauma:

> *"By the waters of Babylon,*
> *there we sat down and wept,*
> *when we remembered Zion.*
> *² On the willows there we hung up our lyres.*
> *³ For there our captors required of us songs,*
> *and our tormentors, mirth, saying,*
> *"Sing us one of the songs of Zion!"*
> *⁴ How shall we sing the LORD's song*
> *in a foreign land?"*[140]

❧❧

As endless days passed for Ezekiel and his Jewish companions in Exile, everything they had believed—about themselves, their heritage, their God—was increasingly called into question. Hope dried up. They could see no future and, therefore, no point to the present. Their lives were empty shells—meaning nothing—waiting for nothing—except, perhaps, to die.

Why am I telling you this? Why am I unpacking all this depressing stuff? Because some of you sitting here or listening on the radio are living lives just like theirs right now. Some of you are looking at a world that is coming apart on you and thinking like Patton, "I'm there." Some of you are wondering how you're going

---

[140] Psalm 137:1-4, RSV.

to get through the day or why you should want to. You're dying inside, and we need to do something about that.

You see, a lot of us who aren't there now have "been there." There are people around you who have lost jobs and fortunes. There are people sitting in this room—you can't imagine how many—who have lost spouses or marriages—who have lost children, or, at least, any chance of relationship with them.

The people who have been there—to some kind of emotional exile from the lives we wanted to live—to "hell on earth"—know there is hope. There is hope and a future for you who are there now—and for those of you who will, some day in the future, feel like everything you care about is gone forever.

What can we do about the misery—the despair—the emptiness you're going through? We can show you what God showed Ezekiel.

Ezekiel said that the hand of God was on him, and the Spirit of God brought him to a place that looked just like they all felt. God took Ezekiel to a place filled with dry, disconnected bones—a bone junkyard. They weren't even skeletons—just bones.

You might call the place the Valley of the Absolutely Lost Cause. God had Ezekiel wander around in this valley of death. He rubbed the Prophet's nose in it—this dead, dry, hopeless place. And then God asked him, *"Can these bones live?"*

Ezekiel dodges the question. As far as he's concerned, there's not a chance in…well, there's not a chance that anything in that valley will ever come even close to living again.

Ezekiel wants to say to God, "Are You crazy? These are dry bones. They have been picked clean and blown dry—dry as dust. There's nothing here but death—old, cold death! Whatever they had—whoever they were—it's over—gone!"

But Ezekiel doesn't say that. He can't bring himself to say "Yes" to God's question, but he doesn't say "No," either. Ezekiel has been a prophet long enough to know that you don't want to put too many things in the "Can't Be Done" column when you're listing what can and can't happen when God is involved. So he simply says, "Pass. I'll let You, God, answer that one."

And God proceeds to do just that. But He does it—God begins to answer His own question—in the affirmative, amazingly—using Ezekiel to do it: "Son of man, prophesy—*to these bones*. In this absolutely hopeless situation, speak for Me to the hopeless situation. Say what I want you to say—what I *command* you to say—to these dry bones. And demand that hopelessness listen to hope."

Today, in your hopeless situation, God *demands* that you hear His word of hope. And just like in Creation, God's word is going to make things exist that don't exist now. God is going to bring things back to life that have no life at all. God doesn't tell you to do "this" or "that." You can't do anything when you've been absolutely wiped out.

God says, "Listen to Me and watch what I'm going to do."

And what you hear is, "I am going to give you your life back. I am going to put your life back together—bit by bit—piece by piece—until you're not destroyed anymore. I'll going to change your situation. I'm going to change your life. I'm going to change you.

"And you will live."

Does Ezekiel believe what God says? We don't know. But he does what he's told to do, as stupid as it seems. Ezekiel stands out there in that valley and prophesies. He speaks the word of God—to bones—dry, dead bones. Ezekiel speaks incredible promises that only a sovereign God can keep. And as he speaks, believing or not, what God tells him to prophesy begins to happen.

God begins doing what He says He will do—He begins putting His people back together. God's powerful promise begins to rattle the bones because it rattles the cage of the evil one who makes it his business to take away hope—to destroy life. God says what He will do, and He does it. And what He does is what is needed to restore hope in the hopeless.

You who sit where you are today, overwhelmed by the disaster your life has become—I declare to you that the God Who put life on this earth in the first place is even now working to put the pieces of your life back together.

Will He take away everything bad and make things just like they were before everything came apart?

No, life was never the same after the Exile as before it. But the dry bones do come back together and the muscles and tendons—the "sinews," God calls them—do connect the bones, and skin does cover these re-formed bodies, because God promised it—and they aren't without hope any more.

೨–◌

But they aren't alive yet, either. It isn't enough to get your life back together when everything in your life has come apart. You need a life that's alive. And to give life to what had been dead, God calls upon Ezekiel for a little more prophecy.

After prophesying to dead bones, Ezekiel's next assignment is to prophesy to God's own Holy Spirit: "Come, Holy Spirit, and put life into people who still don't have it. 'Breathe, O breathe Thy loving Spirit into every troubled breast.'[141] Breathe into every shattered and devastated life that You are putting back together, the spiritual power that will make every person truly alive, to live despite whatever they have lost because they no longer live in their own power—they no longer live without hope, no matter what they've experienced."

With the breath of God's Spirit breathed into you, you are no longer dry bones. You are alive—just like they were in the Garden when God started this whole "form-a-body-and-breathe-into-it-the-breath-of-life" business.[142] And when God makes you alive

---

[141] From Charles Wesley, "Love Divine, All Loves Excelling," Stanza 2, 1747.
[142] Genesis 2:7.

again, you will know that the One Who has made you alive—is God—the only God.

In the Valley of the Dry Bones—the Valley of Absolutely Lost Causes—Ezekiel watches as dry bones come back together and then come back to life. And from there, he takes God's message of life renewed and hope restored back to the Jewish Exiles weeping by the rivers of Babylon: "This Exile will end. This Remnant will return. You who feel like you're dead and just waiting to be buried will be dug up out of your graves and raised to new, real life."

And that's what happened.

⟞⟝

But it didn't stop there.

Just as God the Father was putting people back together through the prophecies of Ezekiel, so Jesus the Son of God was giving life and restoring hope and raising up the dead in His earthly ministry. And the indwelling Holy Spirit is still doing the same thing today—here—for you.

Can't imagine how you will get through what you're going through? Don't imagine yourself getting through it. Imagine Ezekiel prophesying to dry bones that come back to life. Imagine Jesus calling the dead out of their graves. Imagine God doing for you and in you what you could never do yourself.

Whatever it is that's killing you—whatever it is that has robbed you of your hope and joy,

> *"This is what the Sovereign* LORD *says:*
> *'…I am going to open your graves*
> *and bring you up from them…*
> *Then you…will know that I am the* LORD….
> *I will put my Spirit in you and you will live….*
> *Then you will know that I the* LORD *have spoken,*
> *and I have done it, declares the* LORD.'"

Whatever you're going through—God has promised to see that you get through it.

"Now hear the word of the Lord."[143]

ॐ

---

[143] Concluding line to each verse of "Dem Bones," an American spiritual based on Ezekiel 37:1-14, composed by James Weldon Johnson, and first recorded in 1928.

From the Book of Daniel

Daniel 1:1-21 ESV

¹ In the third year of the reign of Jehoiakim king of Judah, Nebuchadnezzar king of Babylon came to Jerusalem and besieged it. ² And the Lord gave Jehoiakim king of Judah into his hand, with some of the vessels of the house of God. And he brought them to the land of Shinar, to the house of his god, and placed the vessels in the treasury of his god. ³ Then the king commanded Ashpenaz, his chief eunuch, to bring some of the people of Israel, both of the royal family and of the nobility, ⁴ youths without blemish, of good appearance and skillful in all wisdom, endowed with knowledge, understanding learning, and competent to stand in the king's palace, and to teach them the literature and language of the Chaldeans. ⁵ The king assigned them a daily portion of the food that the king ate, and of the wine that he drank. They were to be educated for three years, and at the end of that time they were to stand before the king. ⁶ Among these were Daniel, Hananiah, Mishael, and Azariah of the tribe of Judah. ⁷ And the chief of the eunuchs gave them names: Daniel he called Belteshazzar, Hananiah he called Shadrach, Mishael he called Meshach, and Azariah he called Abednego.

⁸ But Daniel resolved that he would not defile himself with the king's food, or with the wine that he drank. Therefore he asked the chief of the eunuchs to allow him not to defile himself. ⁹ And God gave Daniel favor and compassion in the sight of the chief of the eunuchs, ¹⁰ and the chief of the eunuchs said to Daniel, "I fear my lord the king, who assigned your food and your drink; for why should he see that you were in worse condition than the youths who are of your own age? So you would endanger my head with the king." ¹¹ Then Daniel said to the steward whom the chief of the eunuchs had assigned over Daniel, Hananiah, Mishael, and Azariah, ¹² "Test your servants for ten days; let us be given vegetables to eat and water to drink. ¹³ Then let our appearance and the appearance of the youths who eat the king's food be observed by you, and deal with your servants according to what you see." ¹⁴ So he listened to them in this matter, and tested them for ten days. ¹⁵ At the end of ten days it was seen that they were better in appearance and fatter in flesh than all the youths who ate the king's food. ¹⁶ So the steward took away their food and the wine they were to drink, and gave them vegetables.

¹⁷As for these four youths, God gave them learning and skill in all literature and wisdom, and Daniel had understanding in all visions and dreams. ¹⁸At the end of the time, when the king had commanded that they should be brought in, the chief of the eunuchs brought them in before Nebuchadnezzar. ¹⁹And the king spoke with them, and among all of them none was found like Daniel, Hananiah, Mishael, and Azariah. Therefore they stood before the king. ²⁰And in every matter of wisdom and understanding about which the king inquired of them, he found them ten times better than all the magicians and enchanters that were in all his kingdom. ²¹And Daniel was there until the first year of King Cyrus.

છ*~*ઠ

Matthew 15:10-20 ESV

[10] And [Jesus] called the people to him and said to them, "Hear and understand: [11] it is not what goes into the mouth that defiles a person, but what comes out of the mouth; this defiles a person." [12] Then the disciples came and said to him, "Do you know that the Pharisees were offended when they heard this saying?" [13] He answered, "Every plant that my heavenly Father has not planted will be rooted up. [14] Let them alone; they are blind guides. And if the blind lead the blind, both will fall into a pit." [15] But Peter said to him, "Explain the parable to us." [16] And he said, "Are you also still without understanding? [17] Do you not see that whatever goes into the mouth passes into the stomach and is expelled? [18] But what comes out of the mouth proceeds from the heart, and this defiles a person. [19] For out of the heart come evil thoughts, murder, adultery, sexual immorality, theft, false witness, slander. [20] These are what defile a person. But to eat with unwashed hands does not defile anyone."

∂∞∂

19.

Put the Right Stuff In

Daniel 1:1-21; Matthew 15:10-20 ESV

The Book of Daniel is one of the most colorful and exciting books in the Bible. Its pages are filled with political intrigue, dramatic escapes, supernatural encounters and mysterious visions of a troubling future. And it all begins with a crisis over what should be on the menu at the king's training camp for budding bureaucrats.

You know the story. You heard it again just a few minutes ago. Now let's go deeper and see how well you really know it.

Daniel and his friends were the sons of elite families in Judah. They were royal princes—or nearly so. You may imagine what their childhoods were like and the futures they would have enjoyed as the leaders of God's people in the land God had given them. But they were ripped from that heritage and those prospects by an unstoppable foreign invader and carried off into exile, helpless in the hands of their conquerors.

But rather than sadistic torture, or crushing slave labor, or the pointless existence of a subjugated people, the fate in store for these special young men would seem to be miraculous and wonderful: they will be groomed for careers in the administration of the empire.

155

Understand what this means. These boys will spend their lives at the center of political power and the top of economic opportunity. They will travel in the same circles with shakers and movers and eventually do the shaking and moving themselves. It's the chance of a lifetime. They've won the lottery.

But it also means that they have entered another world, one totally alien to the one they grew up in. They will never go home again. They will not even be part of the Jewish community in exile. They will live among and work for those who destroyed their country and their culture, their homes and their hopes—hopes defined by the ancient word of God. The point of the preparation they will undergo is to mold the best and brightest from throughout the empire into the same thing: sons of the empire—servants of the king.

But here's the unspoken question underlying the stories of Daniel and his friends: Can you serve the king and still be God's man? Can you live and work *in* that world, and not be *of* that world? Daniel and his friends believe the answer is "Yes," and they are going to bet their lives on that answer.

The first test comes over something as simple as food—diet. It is simple to the empire, but not to a child of God. What you put in your body determines who you are and how you are relating to God. God has directed what you are to eat. Now you must decide: To whom is your first allegiance to be given when the requirements placed upon you are in conflict?

Daniel's response is not so much to challenge the imperial authority as to suggest that God has given him a better way to achieve the empire's goal. God's way, Daniel urges, is better than the world's way. And when Daniel's conviction is tested practically, he turns out to be right. Living in obedience to God's word *is* the healthiest lifestyle.

The next test is intellectual. Can God's people compete with the wisdom of the world?

Daniel and his friends learn what they have been taught by their imperial instructors about the ways of that world, but God gives them additional and superior insight that cannot be learned in any classroom; it has to be revealed to them by God as a gift to those who are submissive to Him. The king finds them wiser than all their other classmates—and wiser than their instructors, too.

Can a child of God function outside the protective boundaries of the community of faith? The first returns say "Yes," and more: God will cause His faithful follower not merely to survive, but to thrive.

స్తా

Now, fast forward a few hundred years to the time of Jesus.

Jews are scattered all over the Mediterranean world by now, but many are back in the Holy Land God gave them. Jesus is there, talking to people—to His own countrymen and women. He is talking about—teaching them—Who God is and how they are to live in relationship with Him. That's what they've been taught for over a thousand years, but somehow, with Jesus, it's different—new. But some of His countrymen have gone to such extremes in their observance (and enforcement) of dietary restrictions that they are not merely setting themselves apart from the secular world; they are also dividing God's people from each other.

Jesus turns the argument Daniel used around the other way. Jesus addresses a different issue—the unity of God's covenant people—by pointing out that words and deeds have far more impact on your relationship with God and other people than what you fix for dinner or order off the menu.

Religious rituals are valuable as a means to experience and expand your relationship with God—and to share that relationship with those who share your faith—or to explain your faith to those who don't share it. But religious rituals without moral and spiritual realities undergirding them are worthless—and worse: they drive you away from God and from God's people who are genuinely living their faith.

ঔ৽৺

Daniel is determined to put the right stuff in. Jesus demands that you bring the right stuff out. So, are we working at cross purposes here? Perhaps not.

Daniel was determined to put the right stuff in his body—to eat "kosher," even in the heart of the Babylonian bureaucracy. He believed that the right stuff, in terms of superior appearance, health and mental acumen, would come out as a result.

Later, Daniel and his Jewish friends would put their time and their hearts into disciplined (and dangerous) prayer to bring about a stronger relationship with God—and gain the God-given courage to live their faith, sacrificially and victoriously, in the midst of the secular empire and before the political enemies their superior performance—and superior faith—would earn them.

Put the right stuff in, in order to get the right stuff out. It worked for Daniel. It also works with Jesus. In order to get the right stuff out, put the right stuff in.

Jesus says, "What comes out of the heart is a lot more important than what goes into the stomach. *Out of the heart come evil thoughts, murder, adultery, sexual immorality, theft, false testimony, slander. These are what make a man 'unclean.'*"

That's some bad stuff! Why would stuff like that be coming out of our hearts? Because we put it in there in the first place.

Are there evil thoughts coming out of your heart? Then you've probably been listening to evil thoughts—taking them seriously and storing them in your heart. And they come out—sometimes because you bring them out on purpose—sometimes when you don't want them to come out, but you can't control them anymore.

"I haven't murdered anybody!"

But have you wanted to—even a little—even just for an instant? Jesus said anger is the same thing as murder—in the heart.

Do you think all the sexual immorality portrayed and promoted on TV and in the movies and music—all the pornography available on your computer—all the salacious conversations and jokes about sex you hear or take part in don't affect your attitude and resolve about marital fidelity and sexual purity?

We've seen a seismic shift in sexual attitudes and behaviors in our lifetimes, and hearts are not getting cleaner on the diet of depraved sexuality we've been served.

What about theft, lying, slander? When you decide that "things"—possessions, prestige, power—are more important than character, integrity and faithfulness, your heart will send out wicked words and deeds to take what you want and destroy what others have. The more of this world you want—the more of this world you take to heart—the more what will come out of you will not be the right stuff, as God defines it.

❧

When computers started turning up in the workplace and then in homes, many people soon realized that it wasn't always easy to get those new machines to do what you wanted them to do. A pithy term came to sum up the widespread frustration the computers caused: "Garbage in—garbage out."

There is a life application here as well. "Garbage in—garbage out." Put the wrong stuff in—to your stomach or your heart—and you will generally get wrong stuff—undesirable results—out.

Fortunately, there is a divine variation: "gospel in—gospel out." Just as Daniel and his friends were determined to live God-pleasing lives, even as agents of the imperial civil service—so we put things into our hearts and lives as Christians that are pleasing to God, so that what comes out of us will reflect the good news of the gospel of Jesus Christ.

We read the word of God to get it into our hearts and lives— we engage in fellowship with one another—we give ourselves to ministries that extend the touch of Jesus, and devote our time, talents and treasure to the support of God's church and kingdom—we immerse ourselves in prayer and worship—all so that our hearts may be filled with the right stuff of God, and being full, may overflow in word and deed to the glory of God.

No longer do you live in a land where everyone lives (or tries to live) by the law of the Lord. That you will live a life worthy of your calling as a child of God is not a forgone conclusion any more. Putting the right stuff in your body, and in your life, is now an out-of-the-mainstream activity.

But putting the right stuff in is the only way to ensure that the right stuff will come out—the stuff God wants to see in His children.

The world's "garbage" or the Lord's gospel—which will it be?

৯৶৫

Daniel 3:1-30 ESV

The story of the Jewish people for thousands of years has been of their being singled out and persecuted, simply for being Jewish. The story of Shadrach, Meshach and Abednego is one of these stories, telling how some clever (but not wise) enemies think the religious commitment of these three Jewish men can be used as a weapon against them. The story is told in a way that makes fun of the great Babylonian power structure, but the point is deadly serious: true faith is faithful, no matter what it costs the believer.

ॐ⌘

¹ King Nebuchadnezzar made an image of gold, whose height was sixty cubits and its breadth six cubits. He set it up on the plain of Dura, in the province of Babylon. ² Then King Nebuchadnezzar sent to gather the satraps, the prefects, and the governors, the counselors, the treasurers, the justices, the magistrates, and all the officials of the provinces to come to the dedication of the image that King Nebuchadnezzar had set up. ³ Then the satraps, the prefects, and the governors, the counselors, the treasurers, the justices, the magistrates, and all the officials of the provinces gathered for the dedication of the image that King Nebuchadnezzar had set up. And they stood before the image that Nebuchadnezzar had set up. ⁴ And the herald proclaimed aloud, "You are commanded, O peoples, nations, and languages, ⁵ that when you hear the sound of the horn, pipe, lyre, trigon, harp, bagpipe, and every kind of music, you are to fall down and worship the golden image that King Nebuchadnezzar has set up. ⁶ And whoever does not fall down and worship shall immediately be cast into a burning fiery furnace." ⁷ Therefore, as soon as all the peoples heard the sound of the horn, pipe, lyre, trigon, harp, bagpipe, and every kind of music, all the peoples, nations, and languages fell down and worshiped the golden image that King Nebuchadnezzar had set up.

⁸ Therefore at that time certain Chaldeans came forward and maliciously accused the Jews. ⁹ They declared to King Nebuchadnezzar, "O king, live forever! ¹⁰ You, O king, have made a decree, that every man who hears the sound of the horn, pipe, lyre, trigon, harp, bagpipe, and every kind of music, shall fall down and worship the golden image. ¹¹ And whoever does not fall down and worship shall be cast into a burning fiery furnace. ¹² There are certain Jews whom you have appointed over the affairs of the province of Babylon: Shadrach, Meshach, and Abednego. These men, O king, pay no attention to you; they do not serve your gods or worship the golden image that you have set up."

¹³ Then Nebuchadnezzar in furious rage commanded that Shadrach, Meshach, and Abednego be brought. So they brought these men before the king. ¹⁴ Nebuchadnezzar answered and said to them, "Is it true, O Shadrach, Meshach, and Abednego, that you do not serve my gods or worship the golden image that I have set up? ¹⁵ Now if you are ready when you hear the sound of the horn, pipe, lyre, trigon, harp, bagpipe, and every kind of music, to fall down and worship the image that I have made, well and good. But if you do not worship, you shall immediately be cast into a burning fiery furnace. And who is the god who will deliver you out of my hands?"

¹⁶ Shadrach, Meshach, and Abednego answered and said to the king, "O Nebuchadnezzar, we have no need to answer you in this matter. ¹⁷ If this be so, our God whom we serve is able to deliver us from the burning fiery furnace, and he will deliver us out of your hand, O king. ¹⁸ But if not, be it known to you, O king, that we will not serve your gods or worship the golden image that you have set up."

¹⁹ Then Nebuchadnezzar was filled with fury, and the expression of his face was changed against Shadrach, Meshach, and Abednego. He ordered the furnace heated seven times more than it was usually heated. ²⁰ And he ordered some of the mighty men of his army to bind Shadrach, Meshach, and Abednego, and to cast them into the burning fiery furnace. ²¹ Then these men were bound in their cloaks, their tunics, their hats, and their other garments, and they were thrown into the burning fiery furnace. ²² Because the king's order was urgent and the furnace overheated, the flame of the fire killed those men who took up Shadrach, Meshach, and Abednego. ²³ And these three men, Shadrach, Meshach, and Abednego, fell bound into the burning fiery furnace.

²⁴ Then King Nebuchadnezzar was astonished and rose up in haste. He declared to his counselors, "Did we not cast three men bound into the fire?" They answered and said to the king, "True, O king." ²⁵ He answered and

said, *"But I see four men unbound, walking in the midst of the fire, and they are not hurt; and the appearance of the fourth is like a son of the gods."*

²⁶ *Then Nebuchadnezzar came near to the door of the burning fiery furnace; he declared, "Shadrach, Meshach, and Abednego, servants of the Most High God, come out, and come here!" Then Shadrach, Meshach, and Abednego came out from the fire.* ²⁷ *And the satraps, the prefects, the governors, and the king's counselors gathered together and saw that the fire had not had any power over the bodies of those men. The hair of their heads was not singed, their cloaks were not harmed, and no smell of fire had come upon them.* ²⁸ *Nebuchadnezzar answered and said, "Blessed be the God of Shadrach, Meshach, and Abednego, who has sent his angel and delivered his servants, who trusted in him, and set aside the king's command, and yielded up their bodies rather than serve and worship any god except their own God.* ²⁹ *Therefore I make a decree: Any people, nation, or language that speaks anything against the God of Shadrach, Meshach, and Abednego shall be torn limb from limb, and their houses laid in ruins, for there is no other god who is able to rescue in this way."* ³⁰ *Then the king promoted Shadrach, Meshach, and Abednego in the province of Babylon.*

❧❦

Matthew 26:36-42 ESV

Like Shadrach, Meshach and Abednego, Jesus is confronted with the choice of turning away from His commitment to God or losing His life because of it. The story is told in a very different tone, but Jesus, alone in the Garden of Gethsemane, weighs the same options and makes the same choice.

ॐ⬝ᠪ

[36] *Then Jesus went with them to a place called Gethsemane, and he said to his disciples, "Sit here, while I go over there and pray."* [37] *And taking with him Peter and the two sons of Zebedee, he began to be sorrowful and troubled.* [38] *Then he said to them, "My soul is very sorrowful, even to death; remain here, and watch with me."* [39] *And going a little farther he fell on his face and prayed, saying, "My Father, if it be possible, let this cup pass from me; nevertheless, not as I will, but as you will."* [40] *And he came to the disciples and found them sleeping. And he said to Peter, "So, could you not watch with me one hour?* [41] *Watch and pray that you may not enter into temptation. The spirit indeed is willing, but the flesh is weak."* [42] *Again, for the second time, he went away and prayed, "My Father, if this cannot pass unless I drink it, your will be done."*

ॐ⬝ᠪ

20.

But If Not

Daniel 3:1-30; Matthew 26:36-42 ESV

The story of Shadrach, Meshach and Abednego in the third chapter of Daniel makes it very clear that expensive government boondoggles are not a modern development. One day, the great Babylonian king Nebuchadnezzar decided he needed a gold-plated thing-a-ma-jig erected outside the walls of his capital city. So the public works crews got out there and built it.

Then the king decided everybody in the kingdom needed to play "Simon Says" with the thing, so he added a few more government regulations to let people know they would have to *kow-tow* to his image or "participate personally in global warming." He brought in a bunch of big-wigs from all over the empire to brag on him for coming up with such a good idea, and he hired a band to let everybody know when it was time to get down and grovel before his newest pride and joy. Presumably, he also hired extra law enforcement officers to police the process and ensure that everybody played along. Otherwise, somebody might get away with not getting with the mandatory government program.

And sure enough, just when the king seems to have all his ducks (and satraps, prefects and governors) in a row—just when he is finally ready to roll out this wonderful new program and watch everybody in sight (or sound) do "a vertical wave" in response to the "get down" music—a self-appointed Compliance Committee comes along to tell him that Shadrach, Meshach and Abednego aren't going to play along.

Shadrach, Meshach and Abednego don't think the bowing down business is a good idea—even with the musical accompaniment—and they aren't going to do it—no matter what.

Interestingly, the members of the Compliance Committee know this. They know that Shadrach, Meshach and Abednego will not be bowing down, even before the horn, flute, zither, lyre, harp, pipes, etc., crank out the first note. And they are delighted to be able to clue the king in to the egregious non-compliance that is certain to take place.

But how do they know? How do they know that Shadrach, Meshach and Abednego will not be bowing down to the king's image?

They know this because they know that Shadrach, Meshach and Abednego are Jewish. They know Shadrach, Meshach and Abednego don't bow down to images—even gold-plated, skyscraping, government-mandated ones. Shadrach, Meshach and Abednego only bow down to the Real Thing. They only bow down to God.

When you only bow down to God, you're going to be in for a lot of conflict. You see, there are a lot of people who have things they want you to bow down to. A lot of people—in some cases, very powerful people—or very persuasive people—erect their special images and demand that you get on board with whatever they're promoting: "When you hear us singing the praises of this thing or that, you need to 'get with the program'—you need to go along. If you don't, we'll go after *you*. We'll make you sorry. We'll make your life miserable. When you hear 'the music,' you better bow down."

But Shadrach, Meshach and Abednego won't.

They know the difference between God and god-substitutes—even gold-plated ones.

"You'll be sorry!"

"No, we *would* be sorry," say Shadrach, Meshach and Abednego, "if we bowed down to something other than God, just to save our own skins. We may suffer for not bowing down, but we will not be sorry to choose, and serve, and worship, God, rather than anything or anyone set up to compete with God."

And here's where it gets really interesting: This powerful king who has set up this litmus test of loyalty is powerless to compel these seemingly powerless men to comply with his demands. *He* is powerless in the face of their greater loyalty to God. He can throw them into the fire, but he can't get them to bow down. He wants what belongs to God, and these three men of God will not give it to him.

"I'll throw you into the fire! What god can rescue you from me?"

Poor Nebuchadnezzar! He thinks that's a killer argument. He thinks he just won the debate.

"O Nebuchadnezzar," they say, "that's a 'gimme.' *Our* God is able to rescue us from your fiery furnace and from you. We don't know if He will. But that doesn't matter, really.

"What matters to God—and to you, O king—is that we will not bow down to your image. We will not give you what belongs to God alone—no matter what you do to us."

Now, there's more to the story of Shadrach, Meshach and Abednego, but nothing matters as much as what they just told the king: "Our God is able…, but if not, we still will not bow down…!"

�❦�

Flash to another scene of a powerful government official having at a seemingly helpless individual who's run afoul of the law. This time, the power of the Roman Empire is represented in

167

the person of Pontius Pilate, and the One Who will not bow down is Jesus of Nazareth.

Pilate says, *"Don't you realize I have the power either to free You or to crucify You?"*

And Jesus answers, *"You would have no power over Me if it were not given to you from above."*[144]

In other words, "My God is able to rescue Me from you...and I will only bow down to God."

And the evening before, Jesus had done just that, bowing before His Heavenly Father in the dark solitude of Gethsemane and praying, *"if it is possible, may this cup be taken from me... but if not, your will be done."*

Soon after, another self-appointed Compliance Committee came for Jesus, and before too many hours had passed, Jesus was standing before Pilate in the Roman governor's judgment hall with all the trappings of imperial power arrayed around them.

Yet it is Pilate who is powerless before Jesus. Jesus, oddly, is the One with the power in the confrontation between the two. Even when He is tortured and taken to be crucified, Jesus is still the One with the power.

As with the comments of Shadrach, Meshach and Abednego to Nebuchadnezzar, the prayer of Jesus in Gethsemane is not the end of the story. But, again, it is the *point* of the story.

With Shadrach, Meshach and Abednego—as with Jesus—it is the "but-if-not" moment that makes everything else that follows possible. Without that willingness to give God all—whatever the personal cost—knowing what God *can* do, but not knowing what God *will* do—without that willingness to give God all, there is no power to serve God faithfully or survive the pressure to bow down to the endless parade of inferior images the world will erect around you.

---

[144] John 19:10-11, NIV.

The story of Shadrach, Meshach and Abednego is the story of martyrdom—giving up your life for your faith. They would not bow down—and they *were* thrown into the fire. And then they were rescued—miraculously. Most martyrs are not rescued, even today.

Jesus went to the Cross and was crucified. God did not rescue Him. And for that, we say, "Thank You, God!" Because God did not rescue Jesus from His martyrdom on the Cross, you and I *have* been rescued, not from martyrdom, but from a worse fate: the just and eternal punishment for our sins.

Shadrach, Meshach and Abednego were rescued by the mighty hand of God from Nebuchadnezzar's attempt to martyr them. Jesus was not rescued, either from the hands of evil men or the vicious plans of Satan. Remember what Satan said to Jesus in the wilderness temptations, "I will give You all the kingdoms of the world—if You will bow down and worship *me*."[145] What Satan didn't say, but could have, was, "If You don't, I'll see that You'll be tortured to death on a cross."

Jesus' answer was remarkably like Sha—the three guys in Babylon: *"You shall worship the Lord your God and Him only shall you serve.*[146] I will not bow down to your image, whether to avoid the cross or to gain all the kingdoms of the world. I only bow down to God."

Jesus paid the price of His faithfulness to God. He was not rescued.

ॐ♒

Jesus was not rescued, but He was resurrected—and vindicated. And now we know for sure what our God is able to do. Our God is able to deliver us—rescue us—from every thing and every one that would challenge God for supremacy in our lives. Our God is able to protect us from any power that would compel

---

[145] Matthew 4:8-9.
[146] Matthew 4:10, ESV.

us to bow down to anything contrary to God's will. "Halleluiah! There is nothing our God can't do!"

But if not...

Our God is able to cure the disease that's killing you—or someone you love. But if He chooses not to, will you still serve Him? Our God is able to fix your finances. But if not, is He still the One—the only One—you will bow down to? Our God is able to repair your broken relationships. But if He does not, will you continue to believe in Him? Our God is able to put the people you want in office in the upcoming elections. But if He will not do so, will you still trust Him to work His will His way? Our God is able to give you everything you pray for. But if not...?

Can you worship a God—trust a God—love a God—remain loyal to a God—Who does not rescue you from the pain and loss and disappointments you will experience because of your faithfulness to Him? Can you believe that God has a reason for allowing you to suffer the negative consequences of being a follower of Jesus Christ in a world that competes with God every day, in a thousand ways, for your soul?

The reason that you even know the Name of Jesus is that men and women you never knew were willing to pray what Jesus prayed in Gethsemane—were willing to say to their persecutors what Shadrach, Meshach and Abednego said to Nebuchadnezzar: "Whatever you do—whatever God does—I will not bow down to anything that man comes up with. I only bow down to God."

And if men and women, boys and girls in the future, in generations yet unborn, are to know the Name, and the power, of God in Jesus Christ, it will be because you and I and our Christian brothers and sisters around the world in our generation live our lives with a "but if not" faith and conviction.

Your God is able to rescue you from no matter what. Will you worship and serve this God—this God Who has saved you, through the sacrifice of Jesus Christ, no matter what?

Daniel 5:1-31 ESV

¹ King Belshazzar made a great feast for a thousand of his lords and drank wine in front of the thousand.

² Belshazzar, when he tasted the wine, commanded that the vessels of gold and of silver that Nebuchadnezzar his father had taken out of the temple in Jerusalem be brought, that the king and his lords, his wives, and his concubines might drink from them. ³ Then they brought in the golden vessels that had been taken out of the temple, the house of God in Jerusalem, and the king and his lords, his wives, and his concubines drank from them. ⁴ They drank wine and praised the gods of gold and silver, bronze, iron, wood, and stone.

⁵ Immediately the fingers of a human hand appeared and wrote on the plaster of the wall of the king's palace, opposite the lampstand. And the king saw the hand as it wrote. ⁶ Then the king's color changed, and his thoughts alarmed him; his limbs gave way, and his knees knocked together. ⁷ The king called loudly to bring in the enchanters, the Chaldeans, and the astrologers. The king declared to the wise men of Babylon, "Whoever reads this writing, and shows me its interpretation, shall be clothed with purple and have a chain of gold around his neck and shall be the third ruler in the kingdom." ⁸ Then all the king's wise men came in, but they could not read the writing or make known to the king the interpretation. ⁹ Then King Belshazzar was greatly alarmed, and his color changed, and his lords were perplexed.

¹⁰ The queen, because of the words of the king and his lords, came into the banqueting hall, and the queen declared, "O king, live forever! Let not your thoughts alarm you or your color change. ¹¹ There is a man in your kingdom in whom is the spirit of the holy gods. In the days of your father, light and understanding and wisdom like the wisdom of the gods were found in him, and King Nebuchadnezzar, your father—your father the king—made him chief of the magicians, enchanters, Chaldeans, and astrologers, ¹² because an excellent spirit, knowledge, and understanding to interpret dreams, explain riddles, and solve problems were found in this Daniel, whom the king named Belteshazzar. Now let Daniel be called, and he will show the interpretation."

¹³ Then Daniel was brought in before the king. The king answered and said to Daniel, "You are that Daniel, one of the exiles of Judah, whom the king my father brought from Judah. ¹⁴ I have heard of you that the spirit of the gods is in you, and that light and understanding and excellent wisdom are found in you. ¹⁵ Now the wise men, the enchanters, have been brought in before me to read this writing and make known to me its interpretation, but they could not show the interpretation of the matter. ¹⁶ But I have heard that you can give interpretations and solve problems. Now if you can read the writing and make known to me its interpretation, you shall be clothed with purple and have a chain of gold around your neck and shall be the third ruler in the kingdom."

¹⁷ Then Daniel answered and said before the king, "Let your gifts be for yourself, and give your rewards to another. Nevertheless, I will read the writing to the king and make known to him the interpretation. ¹⁸ O king, the Most High God gave Nebuchadnezzar your father kingship and greatness and glory and majesty. ¹⁹ And because of the greatness that he gave him, all peoples, nations, and languages trembled and feared before him. Whom he would, he killed, and whom he would, he kept alive; whom he would, he raised up, and whom he would, he humbled. ²⁰ But when his heart was lifted up and his spirit was hardened so that he dealt proudly, he was brought down from his kingly throne, and his glory was taken from him. ²¹ He was driven from among the children of mankind, and his mind was made like that of a beast, and his dwelling was with the wild donkeys. He was fed grass like an ox, and his body was wet with the dew of heaven, until he knew that the Most High God rules the kingdom of mankind and sets over it whom he will. ²² And you his son, Belshazzar, have not humbled your heart, though you knew all this, ²³ but you have lifted up yourself against the Lord of heaven. And the vessels of his house have been brought in before you, and you and your lords, your wives, and your concubines have drunk wine from them. And you have praised the gods of silver and gold, of bronze, iron, wood, and stone, which do not see or hear or know, but the God in whose hand is your breath, and whose are all your ways, you have not honored."

²⁴ *"Then from his presence the hand was sent, and this writing was inscribed.* ²⁵ *And this is the writing that was inscribed:* MENE, MENE, TEKEL, *and* PARSIN. ²⁶ *This is the interpretation of the matter:* MENE, *God has numbered the days of your kingdom and brought it to an end;* ²⁷ TEKEL, *you have been weighed in the balances and found wanting;* ²⁸ PERES, *your kingdom is divided and given to the Medes and Persians."*

²⁹ *Then Belshazzar gave the command, and Daniel was clothed with purple, a chain of gold was put around his neck, and a proclamation was made about him, that he should be the third ruler in the kingdom.*

³⁰ *That very night Belshazzar the Chaldean king was killed.* ³¹ *And Darius the Mede received the kingdom, being about sixty-two years old.*

৵৽

Matthew 16:1-3 ESV

¹ And the Pharisees and Sadducees came, and to test [Jesus] they asked him to show them a sign from heaven. ² He answered them, "When it is evening, you say, 'It will be fair weather, for the sky is red.' ³ And in the morning, 'It will be stormy today, for the sky is red and threatening.' You know how to interpret the appearance of the sky, but you cannot interpret the signs of the times."

ॐॐ

21.

Wise Ways in Wicked Days

Daniel 5:1-31; Matthew 16:1-3 ESV

The fifth chapter of the Book of Daniel tells about a day in the life of King Belshazzar of Babylon—his last day. It was a day, no doubt, he would have liked to have done over, when all was said and done.

The Bible calls this Belshazzar: "King." But he wasn't, really, according to historical records. The highest he ever got in the kingdom was "regent"—the royal "fill in." Belshazzar got to "pretend" he was a king when his daddy was out of town, which Daddy was a lot, apparently.

One night—his last night—Belshazzar was pretending to be king in a big way. Dad's away—so, obviously (he thought): "Throw a party!" And make it a *king*-sized party—so you can feel like a *real* king. So a thousand big-wigs were brought in to watch Belshazzar wet his whistle with the royal wine.

And then he had an even better idea: "Why not bring out all the gold and silver goblets we swiped from the Temple in Jerusalem when we wiped them out, and we can all drink wine out of these sacred cups while we commit the sacrilege of toasting all the idols that our local god-makers have molded out of metal, wood and stone?"

Well, it seemed like a good idea at the time—as very bad ideas often will to those who don't know any better, and aren't looking at things from God's perspective.

So Belshazzar and his buddies—and a bevy of beauties from his harem, to make things more interesting—filled their glasses for the good time to come—except the gold and silver goblets weren't theirs—they were God's. And on this night, Belshazzar and his buddies went one blasphemy too far.

There were well over two thousand hands there that night, two for every person present.

And then one more hand showed up, and that one hand was all it took to spoil the party. The hand didn't come with a body attached—which was bad enough. But then, instead of grabbing a goblet like all the other hands, this one started writing on the wall, right there in front of Belshazzar.

The Bible doesn't say what Belshazzar did with what was in his hand, but it describes the rest of his reaction in detail: his face went white, his heart skipped a beat (or more), his "loins went loose" (I leave that to your imagination), and his knees were knocking. Fear flooded over him from top to bottom. And that's before he even knew what the hand was writing.

Belshazzar didn't know. None of the big-wigs knew. Nobody in the building could even read the words, much less make out the meaning of the message. But somebody knew somebody who knew somebody who would have a handle on what the hand had written.

The party had gone terribly wrong, so somebody called Belshazzar's momma and she came over and said, "I remember a guy who's good at this sort of stuff. His name's Daniel."

ॐ

Now hold that thought for a minute while we take a brief detour in time and space from Babylon to Egypt and the beginning of the Book of Exodus.

The Book of Exodus begins by saying, *"There arose a new king over Egypt, who did not know Joseph"*[147]—even though Joseph had been the wisest man in Egypt and the most important counselor the pharaohs ever had. That was a thousand years before this party in Babylon, but the parallels between these two wise men are profound.

Daniel had spent a long life advising the kings—the real kings—of Babylon, about stuff only Daniel knew, because Daniel was the only guy God would reveal it to. The Book of Daniel begins with Daniel declining the royal ration of meat and wine when he was a boy starting out his career as a wise man in the Babylonian civil service,[148] which might explain why he wasn't at this blasphemous bash half a century later.

Or, being a smart guy, maybe he knew that he would have found more than the wine unpalatable there. Whatever the reason for his absence, when the night went sour, they sought Daniel out.

But before he looked at the handwriting on the wall, Daniel looked around the room and saw what the horrified people still held in their hands, which prompted a few well-chosen words of wisdom about the folly of what they were doing and why the hand had appeared: "Egregious insults *to* God will not go unnoticed or unpunished *by* God."

❧

The hand from God had written four words: *"MENE, MENE, TEKEL, PARSIN."* It was a foreign language list of descending denominations of money, like: "dollar, dollar, dime and nickel." But the words also sounded like other words—ominous words: "numbered—weighed—divided."

"This is what it says," Daniel told them.

---

147 Exodus 1:8, RSV.
148 Daniel 1.

177

"And this is what it means: God—the God Whose sacred vessels you decided to profane in your sacrilegious ceremony—has numbered your days and those of this kingdom—and both numbers are 'up'! You have been weighed on the scales of significance and found not worth the effort of keeping you alive. Your kingdom—or more accurately, your daddy's—has been divided. And your half is zero."

And sure enough, for Belshazzar, the party, the power to even pretend to be king, and his life were—all—over.

঺৵

Those were wicked days—as are ours. Today, petty kings and queens—pretenders to power in many arenas—flaunt their ability to take the sacred things of God and abuse those things for their own amusement—and to prove that God's faithful servants cannot stop them.

Like Daniel, we live and work in a world that is now foreign to us in many ways. We are aliens in our own land. We labor to do God's will as more and more of our leaders and neighbors take the things we love and cherish and trash them with hedonistic delight. They offer the special things of God Almighty to the lesser gods they worship—and are offended that we are offended when they do.

What are we to do? What is the wise way in these wicked days? Perhaps Daniel has shown us.

Remember, first, that Daniel had to be summoned to the party for the purpose of revealing what no one there knew. He was not a participant in the unholy proceedings. No matter how big the "party of sacrilege" gets, the wise way is to have no part in it.

Daniel spent his whole life in a world he would not have chosen, and he did his best to serve both the system and his God honorably, faithfully and effectively. He would not join "the party," but neither did he go out of his way to court conflict. When men put him in a position where he could not serve God and man both, Daniel did the wise thing: He chose to serve God and trust that God would protect him—or, at least, honor his sacrifice.

And then remember that, one day, God sent the wicked a merciless message: God will not let the godless "party on" forever, in defiance of His holiness.

The handwriting may, already, be "on the wall" for us. Every day, there is more and more to terrify anyone willing to see it. But the wicked blind themselves to God's wisdom because they are so enamored of their own. Who can see (and recognize) what judgment God has written in the unfolding events of our time?

The truth is that God has already written His message for the world in rebellion against Him. It exists in what has become a foreign language—a forgotten language—for many.

But not for us. We read God's word every day. We make sure we know what God says.

Daniel told Belshazzar what God's words on the wall said. He was the only one wise enough to know—because God had made him wise. Knowing God's word makes you wise in wicked times.

Daniel knew what God said—and he knew what God meant: "numbered, weighed, divided." It is a terrifying judgment. But what other verdict can there be upon those who ignore the divinely inspired lessons of the past and will not honor the God Whose hand holds our every breath?

❦

Wise ways in wicked days?

Skip the parties the powerful pretenders put on. Make yourself ever more familiar with the language of God. Understand that God's word contains God's message for our time, every bit as much as it did for Daniel's. Be prepared to share the message with the "Belshazzars" of our day when the work of God's hand scares them enough, finally, to make them want to know what God is saying to them.

For Belshazzar, it was too late by the time he saw the handwriting on the wall. Perhaps it will not be for those risking God's wrath today.

After all, an unnamed thief saw the handwriting on a Cross on *his* last day on earth, and he's been celebrating with a real King—the King of kings—ever since.[149]

Wise man.

৵৽

---

[149] Luke 23:38-43.

From the Book of Hosea

Hosea 5:15—6:6 ESV

[God said to Hosea:]
> *5* *¹⁵* *"I will return again to my place,*
>> *until they acknowledge their guilt and seek my face,*
>> *and in their distress earnestly seek me."*

[The people said:]
> *6* *¹* *"Come, let us return to the* LORD;
>> *for he has torn us, that he may heal us;*
>> *he has struck us down, and he will bind us up.*
> *² After two days he will revive us;*
>> *on the third day he will raise us up,*
>> *that we may live before him.*
> *³ Let us know; let us press on to know the* LORD;
>> *his going out is sure as the dawn;*
>> *he will come to us as the showers,*
>>> *as the spring rains that water the earth."*

[God said to the people:]
> *⁴ "What shall I do with you, O Ephraim?*
>> *What shall I do with you, O Judah?*
>> *Your love is like a morning cloud,*
>>> *like the dew that goes early away."*

[God said to Hosea:]
> *⁵ "Therefore I have hewn them by the prophets;*
>> *I have slain them by the words of my mouth,*
>> *and my judgment goes forth as the light.*
> *⁶ For I desire steadfast love and not sacrifice,*
>> *the knowledge of God rather than burnt offerings."*

る~ら

183

Philippians 3:7-11 ESV

⁷ But whatever gain I had, I counted as loss for the sake of Christ. ⁸ Indeed, I count everything as loss because of the surpassing worth of knowing Christ Jesus my Lord. For his sake I have suffered the loss of all things and count them as rubbish, in order that I may gain Christ ⁹ and be found in him, not having a righteousness of my own that comes from the law, but that which comes through faith in Christ, the righteousness from God that depends on faith— ¹⁰ that I may know him and the power of his resurrection, and may share his sufferings, becoming like him in his death, ¹¹ that by any means possible I may attain the resurrection from the dead.

ॐॐ

22.

It's Who You Know

Hosea 5:15—6:6; Philippians 3:7-11 ESV

The old saying goes, "It's not *what* you know; it's *who* you know." Whatever you're trying to accomplish, it implies, your associations are more important than your abilities. Better to depend on your interpersonal network than your individual merits.

And cynical as it sounds, it's often right. And it's *absolutely* right regarding matters of ultimate reality. When it comes to heaven, hell and the living of this life, Who you know matters more than anything else.

Unfortunately, more and more people today not only don't know the right "Who," they don't even know the "what" that will help them meet the "Who" they need to know more than anybody else.

The "Who" they need to know—we all need to know—is God. That's what the prophets and the apostles were saying in Bible times, and that truth hasn't changed. The Prophet Hosea knew that too many people knew too many other gods at a time when his country was coming apart and needing all the holy help it could get.

The people in charge of the country were putting their faith in all the wrong "whos," hoping that hasty alliances with other countries, large and small, would keep them safe from threats they could not overcome themselves. And the people themselves spent their time celebrating all the other gods, assuming that, when it comes to things religious, "the more, the merrier."

This seemed like a good plan because they had forgotten Who got them where they were in the first place: the divine Who Who had also been giving them all the good things they had enjoyed ever since. They no longer knew their own God, and what was happening all around them was the proof.

God said, through Hosea,

> *"There is no faithfulness or steadfast love,*
> *and no knowledge of God in the land....*
> *My people are destroyed for lack of knowledge."*[150]

And Hosea saw the similarity between Israel's unfaithfulness to her God and that of his own despicable wife to himself. His wife didn't have a clue or a care about loving her husband with true covenant devotion. And God's people didn't treat their Lord any better.

Oh, when their political and economic situation "went south," the people sang the old religious songs:

> *"Come, let us return to the LORD...*
> *he will heal us...he will bind us up...*
> *he will revive us and raise us up...*
> *he will come to us for sure."*

Sounds like all the people who showed up in all the churches after 9/11 shook everybody up so bad: "Come, let us return to the Lord—for a couple of weeks, until we feel better—for a little while, until we see if anything else bad is going to happen."

But God is not impressed with puny gestures of religious practice. You see, knowing God, which is what God wants from us, isn't just coming to church once in a while (though coming to church is something I would not discourage as a rule). Knowing

---

[150] Hosea 4:1, 6, ESV.

God is not putting money in the plate—even in sacrificial sums (though the ministries of the church do require financial support).

What God wants is true, God-like love and the kind of "knowing" that comes from an interactive, personal relationship that is far deeper than detached theological thinking and religious rituals performed by rote. Drawing on Hosea's marriage imagery, God says to His unfaithful people,

"I will betroth you to me
forever.
I will betroth you to me
in righteousness and in justice,
in steadfast love and in mercy.
I will betroth you to me
in faithfulness.
And you shall know the LORD."[151]

ॐ

Why is "knowing God" so absolutely vital?

God is the One Who punishes us when we are sinful—the One Who causes us to reap what we sow. God is too dangerous *not* to know!

And God is the One—the only One—Who can heal us and save us when we are, otherwise, totally lost and completely destroyed. God is the only One Who can do for us what must ultimately be done for us.

God knows *us*, certainly. He knew us before we were conceived[152] and has had complete and perfect knowledge of us every moment of our lives.[153] God knows us infinitely better than we know ourselves.[154]

---

[151] Hosea 2:19-20, ESV.
[152] Psalm 139:13; Jeremiah 1:5.
[153] Matthew 10:29-31.
[154] Psalm 39:4.

But how are we to know God in the way that He wants us to know Him?

We can only know what He is willing for us to know—what He chooses to reveal of Himself to us.[155] Of that, God will cause us—help us—to know as much as we are willing to know—all that we seek to know about Him.[156] Read your Bible. Pray. Listen to sermons. Share in fellowship and perform ministry. These activities will help, but they are not the goal.

God wants you to know Him directly—personally—and He will not be satisfied until you do. To make that possible, God *"emptied himself…taking the form of a servant, being born in the likeness of men."*[157] And so, it is possible to know God now in a way that Hosea hardly could have conceived.

Please understand: Knowing *about* God is not *knowing* God. The Apostle Paul knew all about God. Everything his Bible said about God, Paul had studied carefully and committed to memory, so he could do exactly what God wanted Him to do—except Paul didn't know God well enough to know that knowing *about* God wasn't what God wanted from him at all. Paul thought it was all about *"what* you know."

And then, Paul met God in the person of Jesus Christ and, in Christ, he finally got to know God the way God wants to be known. It's not *what* you know; it's *Who* you know. And when Paul realized that he could, finally, truly know God, that's all he ever wanted from then on.

He called it *"the surpassing worth of knowing Christ Jesus my Lord."*

To know someone, you have to meet him, spend time with him, communicate with him, observe him in many situations, come to trust him. You become close, understanding his character, values and goals. You dedicate yourself to your part of the relationship.

---

[155] Deuteronomy 29:29.
[156] Isaiah 55:6; James 1:5-6.
[157] Philippians 2:7, ESV.

A relationship as demanding as the Prophet Hosea saw marriage to be—and "knowing God" to be—is actually more demanding than going through a routine of church rituals. But then again, you can't get what you truly need from God by trying to butter Him up a little with a few visits to His house[158] and a few coins in His coffers.[159] That's the kind of love that dissolves like the dew at dawn, and God surely knows the difference.

Paul found that he came to know God best by sharing in the sufferings of Christ. That's a love that doesn't melt away like the morning mist. And in that faithfulness that would not let go of the God Who would not let go of him,[160] Paul found that he was being formed into the likeness of Christ, that he had come to know the God-Who-was-Christ so well that, with the Holy Spirit's help, he could imitate Christ in his own life—and death.

৵৽৾

We began by talking about what a failing country needed to do to get back on track and save itself from the coming catastrophe its own faithlessness had caused. The simple truth is that, at any point in history, it will take a people who come to realize that the secret to social and spiritual salvation lies not in *what* they know, but in *Who* they know—people willing to know that Who—and love that Who—and submit themselves in humility and repentance to that Who, with the total dedication He demands.

So let us conclude with the critical question: "Do *you*...know *Who*?"

৵৽৾

---

158 Amos 5:21.
159 Amos 4:4-5.
160 Romans 8:38-39.

From the Book of Amos

Amos 5:4, 7, 10, 21-24 ESV

[4] *For thus says the* LORD *to the house of Israel:*
"Seek me and live;

[7] *"O you who turn justice to wormwood*
and cast down righteousness to the earth!

[10] *"They hate him who reproves in the gate,*
and they abhor him who speaks the truth.

[21] *"I hate, I despise your feasts,*
and I take no delight in your solemn assemblies.
[22] *Even though you offer me*
your burnt offerings and grain offerings,
I will not accept them;
and the peace offerings of your fattened animals,
I will not look upon them.
[23] *Take away from me the noise of your songs;*
to the melody of your harps I will not listen."

[24] *"But let justice roll down like waters,*
and righteousness like an ever-flowing stream."

૭ૐ

23.

Religion, Inside and Out

Amos 5:4, 7, 10, 21-24 ESV

One day, a stranger showed up in town. He was a troublemaker—a *religious* troublemaker. Religion was big business in the town and business was booming. But it wasn't long before the stranger had trouble brewing with the leaders of the religion in town. He was telling everybody in town that the religion in town wasn't right. That kind of criticism is not good for business—if your business is religion. But the stranger didn't seem to care what his words were doing to business. He was a troublemaker, all right.

The leaders of the religion business in the town tried to reason with the stranger: "Shut up!" they explained.[161] But this kind of reasoning didn't work on the stranger. He just kept on stirring up trouble. "Your religion is messed up," he said.

"What are you talking about? People are pouring in for our religious programs. The place where we do religion is packed. The collection plates are piled high with offerings. The air is filled with the sweet smoke of sacrifices and the sound of religious songs. Everybody is happy with their religious experience."

"Everybody but God," replied the stranger.

---

[161] A slight paraphrase of a line of dialogue by Ring Lardner, *The Young Immigrunts*, Indianapolis, IN: The Bobbs-Merrill Company, 1920, p. 78.

And that kind of talk just stirs up trouble, because the point of religion, after all—to put it in "business" terms—is to make God happy—so *you* can be happy. And the people running the religion business in town had assured everybody that their religion business would make God happy. Guaranteed. "You give us your religion business, and you can go home happy."

And then a stranger showed up and said, "Don't you believe it. God is *not* happy." And people hearing that—whether they're on their way in or on their way out—are a lot less happy than they were before they heard it.

So what was the problem? Why was this stranger stirring up trouble about their religion?

The problem was that religion—religion that makes God happy—is not just an "inside" business. It's not just a matter of going inside a religious place on a religious day and doing the religious things—like preaching, praying, singing, and sacrificing—that religious leaders tell you you're supposed to do.

The leaders in town had that part of the business—"inside religion"—the religious ritual—down cold: one place, one day of the week, one religious routine for everybody to go through. Check the block and click your heels and you were "home free"—as far as God was concerned.

Except you weren't, according to the annoying, troublemaking stranger. Right religion—religion that works—religion that makes this particular God happy—and so can really make you happy, and not just deceived—is a religion that has two components: the inside part of religion that was so big in town, and the outside part that, it turns out, the business of religion in town was totally ignoring.

It turns out that what people do the other six days of the week in all the other places they go with all the other people they meet is also part of this religion. And it turns out that you have to make God happy inside and out before God is going to be happy with your religion.

Inside, it's singing and praying and putting your money in the plate and your arms around the people around you.

Outside, in the big, bad world with all the people you don't know, it's seeking God in everything going on, with a passion as great as you bring to worship, and doing whatever you do so that the impact on everybody else is fair and right.

Get one part of religion right and not the other, and even the one part that seems right won't be making God happy. The religious songs weren't right because the people singing them on "religion day" were sticking it to the poor every other day. Their prayers were as offensive to God as the schemes they were cooking up during the rest of the week to get around the system.

Ya gotta do religion right, inside and out, if you're gonna make God happy.

These days, people want to ignore the inside component and focus on the outside. Forget the church; just be nice. Help the poor and support all the causes that get lumped in the general category of "social justice." Unfortunately, when you abandon organized religion, what you have left is bound to be dis-organized—chaos— "anarchy of the soul."[162] You bet your life that there is no God Whose displeasure you need to consider, or that the God Who does exist—the divine Stranger you do not know and are not trying to meet—will be satisfied with the fading fragment of inside religion you have chosen to keep clutching, independent of His will or enabling power.

Do not confuse your self-supplied sense of moral superiority with divine approval. The "outside" dimension without the "inside" is just as unacceptable to God as the other way around.

How do you know?

Well, just as a personal dedication to the practice of religious rituals without a commitment to a just society does not of itself ensure divine protection and prosperity, so obviously, God has not

---

[162] I do not know the origin of this phrase, but found it very useful for describing life apart from Christ.

blessed the slavish devotion to programs of public morality on the part of those devoid of personal faith with the advent of the utopian society they seek.

ॐॐ

There are two dimensions to religion that is pleasing to God: the inside and the outside. There is what we do inside the church and what we do outside, in the world. That's what the stranger in town was saying. And the reason that what he said stirred up so much trouble—and still does—is that human nature—human depravity—makes all of us want to choose one part over the other when it comes to religion. We want God to be satisfied with either our personal piety or our public service. We don't want God to hold us equally responsible for both.

"Lord, I'm totally committed to Your church. Can't I let the world fend for itself?" Or, "Look, I'm out there helping people all the time. I ought to be able to do whatever I want in my private life without anybody telling me it's wrong."

But, friends, it just doesn't work that way, whatever side you want to come down on. On this, God is not flexible.

And why is it that God demands that we engage with Him in both dimensions of religion?

I think it has to do with that "Greatest Commandment" thing. Do you remember how it goes?

> *"Thou shalt love the Lord thy God*
> *with all thy heart*
> *and with all thy soul*
> *and with all thy mind.*
> *This is the first and great commandment.*
> *And the second is like unto it:*
> *thou shalt love thy neighbor as thyself."*[163]

---

[163] Matthew 22:37-39, KJV. Also included in the communion liturgy of *The Episcopal Book of Common Prayer*, 1928.

God created us to love Him. The inside component of religion is the place and time and process in which we come as individuals into the holy presence of God and express our love for Him. Because we love God, we want to know Him better and to get closer to Him. We want to engage more of ourselves in our relationship with Him—our hearts, our souls and our minds.

We communicate in prayer, we celebrate in song, we open a window within us to His revelation of Himself as we read His word and hear it proclaimed. We give of our physical possessions sacrificially to show our desire to give Him our spirits—our selves.

If we do not seek God, we do not love Him. If we do not live in an actively loving relationship with Him, we cannot live as He created us to live, which means that we cannot truly live, because God is not willing for us to live any other way. Without God's presence with us and within us, by our invitation and submission, we are merely creatures whose spirits are decomposing day by day, just as our bodies will do someday, when God no longer enables our physical existence on this earth.

Our ever-growing, ever-maturing love relationship with God is the purpose and the product of the inner dimension of our religion. But God also created us to love the things and the people that He loves—that He created in love just like He created us. "Seek Me and live," God said. But He also said, "Seek justice! Seek righteousness!"

When we seek the wellbeing of other people, especially those who are innocent or defenseless, those who are in need and cannot repay our kindness—when we seek to structure our society as a level playing field and to manage our communities and our world as responsible stewards—when we do these things, we are loving our neighbor as ourselves, and making God happy in the process, as happy as all our prayers and praises and presence in church make Him. We are fulfilling the outward component of the religion to which God has called us and for which He holds us accountable.

෧⊷෧

One day, another Stranger showed up in another town—a big religion town—perhaps the biggest of all. Right away, the Stranger started making trouble for that town's religion business.

He wasn't against religion. He just came to tell the people in charge of the business and those participating in the business that the business wasn't right—because *they* weren't right, inside or out.

They tried to shut Him up, this troublemaking Stranger Who seemed so bad for their religion business. And they thought they had, for about three days. And then they found out two things: They found out that this Stranger was actually the official, worldwide Inspector of religion, sent out from the headquarters in the home office with orders from the very Top to find and fix what was wrong with the religion business in that town and every town—which the Stranger did.

They also found out that they would never be able to shut Him up. He just kept going from town to town, to every person participating in religion and all those who weren't, saying,

"Seek ye first the kingdom of God—and his righteousness..."[164] "Love God... Love your neighbor..."

"Inside" religion and "outside" religion. It takes both. Saving faith and selfless service, by the grace of God and for His glory.

৵৽

---

[164] Matthew 6:33, KJV.

From the Book of Jonah

Jonah 1:1-16 ESV

¹ Now the word of the LORD came to Jonah the son of Amittai, saying, ² "Arise, go to Nineveh, that great city, and call out against it, for their evil has come up before me."

³ But Jonah rose to flee to Tarshish from the presence of the LORD. He went down to Joppa and found a ship going to Tarshish. So he paid the fare and went down into it, to go with them to Tarshish, away from the presence of the LORD.

⁴ But the LORD hurled a great wind upon the sea, and there was a mighty tempest on the sea, so that the ship threatened to break up. ⁵ Then the mariners were afraid, and each cried out to his god. And they hurled the cargo that was in the ship into the sea to lighten it for them. But Jonah had gone down into the inner part of the ship and had lain down and was fast asleep.

⁶ So the captain came and said to him, "What do you mean, you sleeper? Arise, call out to your god! Perhaps the god will give a thought to us, that we may not perish."

⁷ And they said to one another, "Come, let us cast lots, that we may know on whose account this evil has come upon us." So they cast lots, and the lot fell on Jonah. ⁸ Then they said to him, "Tell us on whose account this evil has come upon us. What is your occupation? And where do you come from? What is your country? And of what people are you?"

⁹ And he said to them, "I am a Hebrew, and I fear the LORD, the God of heaven, who made the sea and the dry land." ¹⁰ Then the men were exceedingly afraid and said to him, "What is this that you have done!" For the men knew that he was fleeing from the presence of the LORD, because he had told them.

¹¹ Then they said to him, "What shall we do to you, that the sea may quiet down for us?" For the sea grew more and more tempestuous.

¹² He said to them, "Pick me up and hurl me into the sea; then the sea will quiet down for you, for I know it is because of me that this great tempest has come upon you." ¹³ Nevertheless, the men rowed hard to get back to dry land, but they could not, for the sea grew more and more tempestuous against them.

¹⁴ *Therefore they called out to the* LORD, *"O* LORD, *let us not perish for this man's life, and lay not on us innocent blood, for you, O* LORD, *have done as it pleased you."*

¹⁵ *So they picked up Jonah and hurled him into the sea, and the sea ceased from its raging.* ¹⁶ *Then the men feared the* LORD *exceedingly, and they offered a sacrifice to the* LORD *and made vows.*

ॐ•ॐ

Matthew 8:23-27 ESV

²³ *And when [Jesus] got into the boat, his disciples followed him.* ²⁴ *And behold, there arose a great storm on the sea, so that the boat was being swamped by the waves; but he was asleep.* ²⁵ *And they went and woke him, saying, "Save us, Lord; we are perishing." ²⁶ And he said to them, "Why are you afraid, O you of little faith?" Then he rose and rebuked the winds and the sea, and there was a great calm.* ²⁷ *And the men marveled, saying, "What sort of man is this, that even winds and sea obey him?"*

❧

24.

When You Think You're Going Under

Jonah 1:1-16; Matthew 8:23-27 ESV

Two boats—two unexpected, monster storms—two men sleeping peacefully while everyone else on board the two boats are in a panic, certain they are all of them going to die.

Two men who, when awakened, get up and "shut down" the respective storms, saving their companions and showing the incredible power of God—over the natural world and human life.

❧

Jonah and Jesus—you wouldn't expect to find a more unlikely pair for comparison, and yet Matthew, Mark and Luke seem determined to make them so—to compare and contrast them—because they wouldn't have told the story of Jesus calming His storm the way they did if they didn't want you to see Jonah and his stormy boat ride in the background.

So let's start with Jonah. The commonalities, we've already mentioned. The contrasts will also be instructive. Jonah is a prophet of God who doesn't want to prophesy for God. Jonah hates his enemies and hopes they get everything they've got coming—everything God can do to them except what God wants to do to them, which is to forgive them, though God knows as well as Jonah they don't deserve it. Jonah wants to call down God's wrath on his enemies. God wants to shower them with blessings. But reconciliation with God requires repentance of sin, and for his enemies to know that, Jonah will have to tell them, which is the last thing he wants to do.

So Jonah, who is prophet enough to know better than to prophesy something other than God's word, goes AWOL, hoping to get out of saying anything at all. He takes a boat in the opposite direction from where God wants him to go, and soon discovers— along with everybody else on board—that the God Who put the waters in their place at Creation can pile them up on a little boat if He wants to.

Jonah discovers that disobeying God can bring danger on himself and others. And to save those others from the trouble he has caused, Jonah realizes he must give himself up to the God of sea and storm. The salvation of everyone else in the boat depends on his sacrificing himself for them. And self-centered Jonah, who seems a lot calmer "taking his medicine" *from* God than he was about relaying a message *for* God, calms the storm by his heroic act of self-sacrifice.

We didn't read far enough for you to hear it, but if you remember your Bible stories, you know that God did not waste Jonah's sacrifice. Jonah did not die. He was swallowed by a great fish and spit out again three days later, to go do what God had intended him to do in the first place.

∂∾◦∾

And then there's Jesus, Who, at one point, tells His critics that the only sign or proof they're going to get of His being the Messiah is something He calls *"the sign of Jonah,"*[165] which isn't exactly crystal clear, even when He says it. So even Jesus is thinking about Jonah *some* of the time. And maybe one of those times is when Jesus gets

---

[165] Luke 11:29-30.

in a boat with His disciples in tow to go across some water *to* (rather than away *from*) where God wants Him to go. Exhausted, not from opposition to God, but from a radical obedience to His Heavenly Father, Jesus curls up in the stern of the boat and sleeps, trusting perhaps in the superior seamanship of the fishermen among His disciples: Peter, Andrew, James and John.[166]

But storms come, even when Jesus is in the boat. He is the Christ, not a meteorological good luck charm.

The disciples man the helm and work the sails. They bail for dear life and then despair of even that as the waters rush in around them and the boat sinks ever lower in the sea. And then, finally, they call out to Jesus—present Jesus—powerful Jesus—sleeping Jesus:

> *"Master, Master, we're going to drown!"*
> *"Lord, save us! We're going to drown!"*
> *"Teacher, don't You care if we drown?"*[167]

The wording is a little different in each Gospel; they really didn't have the time or the inclination to agree on a unified message. "Teacher—Master—Lord! We're going to drown!"

"Don't You *care*? *Save* us!"

"*Save* us!" That's what they said to Jonah, if not in so many words. "You know what's going on. You know what needs to be done. Please! We're going under!"

And the two men of God get up and save their shipmates. Jonah, the disobedient servant, gives himself up to God, Who brought the storm to stop Jonah's escape from Him. But Jesus, the always obedient Son of God, has no need to right a wrong in His relationship with His Heavenly Father.

And the storm, in His case, is not God's doing. It is a natural phenomenon—or perhaps something more sinister, if the words Jesus uses on the storm are any indication.

---

[166] Matthew 4:18, 21.
[167] Luke 8:24; Matthew 8:25; Mark 4:38, NIV.

When Jesus gets up, He speaks with the authority of God as He always does, and the words He uses are the same words He will use to command the demons to come out of those who are possessed. Jesus rebukes the wind and waves as He would—and has—the devil himself.

The winds roar and Jesus roars back, "Quiet!" The waves slap the boat like a baby's bath toy and Jesus demands of them like a stern parent, "Be still!" And He is obeyed as quickly and completely as He obeys God His Father.

The disciples were terrified by the storm that would surely have destroyed them. Now they are terrified—and more—by the Man Who destroyed the storm. The sea is calm and the wind is a whisper and the Man Who calmed the storm is now turning His attention to them.

"Why are you so afraid?" He asks, perturbed. So where do you point? At the storm that isn't there anymore—or at Him Who is very, *very* "there"?

"Where is your faith?" He says, and turns to go back to His seat in the stern of the boat—and perhaps back to sleep if there is time before they reach the shore.

But for the disciples, there will be no sleep on this trip. They've got some things to "process." "What kind of Man is This?" What kind of Man speaks to a gale and it goes away? What kind of Man wills a wall of water into submission with a word? What are we dealing with here?

Jonah was a man of God who knew what people needed to do to be saved from God's wrath. Okay. Understood.

But Jesus is…*what*? A Man Who has the authority to exercise God's power personally to control Creation and save His followers from the storm. It could be a scary thing to have that kind of power hanging around. But when you think you're going under, Who do you want in your boat?

And speaking of your boat, you need to know that, in the Gospels, boats are usually also symbols for the Church. Just as you look at Jesus in this boat in the storm and see the shadow of Jonah in the background, so the early Christians looked at the disciples in the boats of the New Testament and saw themselves in the future.

As the Church, they, too, were in a vessel tossed about by the storms of life, buffeted by the winds of hostility and drenched by waves of persecution. Without Jesus, they were unproductive in their purpose. The disciples in their fishing boats caught no fish without the help of Jesus. Christians draw in no converts without His help and direction, either. Without Him, the little boat of the Church was always at risk.

But Jesus *was* with them—in the boat—amid the storms. If they ignored Him and tried to sail the boat by themselves, they often stirred up their own storms. And He lay asleep—dormant—whatever the problem.

But when they called upon Him, He rose and rebuked the terrifying storms like the evil things they were. Time and time again, Jesus saved them, the disciples in the boat—the Christians in the Church.

And He still does.

Yes, the storms of life are real. None of us escape them. Some of you are bailing out and battening down for all you're worth—right now. How will you survive the storm? How will you ever keep from going under?

Call on the One Who has the power to put every storm in its place. Reach out to the Savior you so often forget until the tempest rages around you and you can see no way to safety.

And remember that you have followed Jesus into a special boat for the spiritual journey He has invited you to share. You and those who share this boat with you are not adrift in the sea; you are not helpless or deserted, left to face the storms of life alone. There is a Savior in this boat—there is a Captain Who is able to preserve His vessel from all hazards—Who can keep you from falling, and bring you safely home.

Why do we care so much about *this* boat—this fellowship—this church?

Because this is *our* boat—the boat Jesus has called us to sail in through the churning, treacherous waters of our day. It is our vessel of safety amid all the storms—the vessel where Jesus is with us—where Jesus will rise up and rebuke everything that would overwhelm us and pull us under.

Our church is the holy vessel where our faith in Him overcomes our fear of the world and what it can do to us without His divine power to protect us.

༺﹒༻

For almost a thousand years, churches in many countries have hung models of ships in their sanctuaries as a reminder of this biblical symbolism. There is a boat suspended even now high above the balcony of the Naval Academy Chapel in Annapolis. A cable connects it to the ceiling, and seemingly, to heaven.

And so are we connected. Our little boat—this fellowship—afloat on the great and perilous sea—is connected to heaven by the One Who calms the seas for all who sail in faith together in the vessel He has provided.

I learned in that Naval Academy Chapel many years ago to sing,

> "O hear us when we cry to Thee
> for those in peril on the sea."[168]

Little did I know at the time that it was a prayer, not just for sailors, but for you and me and all those saved by the grace and power of Jesus.

Thank God the winds and waves of life obey Him. Thank God our Savior answers that prayer for us.

༺﹒༻

---

[168] William Whiting, "Eternal Father, Strong to Save," 1860.

From the Book of Micah

Micah 6:6-8 ESV

⁶ With what shall I come before the LORD,
and bow myself before God on high?
Shall I come before him with burnt offerings,
with calves a year old?
⁷ Will the LORD *be pleased*
with thousands of rams,
with ten thousands of rivers of oil?
Shall I give my firstborn for my transgression,
the fruit of my body for the sin of my soul?

⁸ He has told you, O man, what is good;
and what does the LORD *require of you*
but to do justice, and to love kindness,
and to walk humbly with your God?

෩෧

Matthew 18:23-35 ESV

[Jesus said:]

²³ "Therefore the kingdom of heaven may be compared to a king who wished to settle accounts with his servants. ²⁴ When he began to settle, one was brought to him who owed him ten thousand talents. ²⁵ And since he could not pay, his master ordered him to be sold, with his wife and children and all that he had, and payment to be made. ²⁶ So the servant fell on his knees, imploring him, 'Have patience with me, and I will pay you everything.' ²⁷ And out of pity for him, the master of that servant released him and forgave him the debt. ²⁸ But when that same servant went out, he found one of his fellow servants who owed him a hundred denarii, and seizing him, he began to choke him, saying, 'Pay what you owe.' ²⁹ So his fellow servant fell down and pleaded with him, 'Have patience with me, and I will pay you.' ³⁰ He refused and went and put him in prison until he should pay the debt. ³¹ When his fellow servants saw what had taken place, they were greatly distressed, and they went and reported to their master all that had taken place. ³² Then his master summoned him and said to him, 'You wicked servant! I forgave you all that debt because you pleaded with me. ³³ And should not you have had mercy on your fellow servant, as I had mercy on you?' ³⁴ And in anger his master delivered him to the jailers, until he should pay all his debt. ³⁵ So also my heavenly Father will do to every one of you, if you do not forgive your brother from your heart."

ॐ•ॐ

25.

Let's Take a Walk

Micah 6:6-8; Matthew 18:23-35 ESV

Have you ever thought about how much walking they do in the Bible? Yes, I know that mass transit had not been invented yet and there weren't nearly enough moderately priced camels, donkeys, carts and chariots to go around. But, even so, the Bible talks an awful lot about "walking."

You start out with God walking in the Garden of Eden in *"the cool of the day."*[169] And then, Abraham and Sarah and their people walk into Canaan in obedience to God's will[170]—only to have their great-grandson, Joseph, walk out of it, into Egypt, against his will.[171]

Centuries later, the significantly expanded Hebrew people walk out of Egypt, through divinely parted waters, as slaves miraculously delivered,[172] only to walk around the desert for 40 years,[173] before walking back into Canaan to claim it as their God-given home.[174]

---

[169] Genesis 3:8, KJV.
[170] Genesis 12:4-6.
[171] Genesis 37:28.
[172] Exodus 14:21-31.
[173] Numbers 32:13.
[174] Joshua 1:11.

In the New Testament, Jesus walked all over Galilee where He grew up, preaching the gospel.[175] And then He walked right through Samaria[176]—which most people made sure they walked around—and He preached the gospel there.[177] And then He walked all the way to Jerusalem, all the while knowing the important people in the capital city were going to kill Him because He was preaching the gospel.[178]

❧

But not all of the hundreds of references to walking in the Bible are talking about literal, physical walking. "Walking" in the Bible often refers to behavior—whether you do right or do wrong. And how you "walk" in this moral, spiritual sense has a lot to do with your relationship with God. *"Enoch walked with God"* in this sense, it says.[179] Enoch was the great-great-great-great-grandson of Adam, who was himself too afraid to come out and walk with God, as he used to, after he and Eve ate the forbidden fruit.[180]

But Enoch's great-grandson, Noah, like Enoch, did walk with God.[181] Though, for a while, the only place he could walk with God was around the deck of the ark God had him build. And even there, he had to be careful where he stepped.

But walking with God is always about watching where you step. God told Moses in the wilderness, *"...make them know the way in which they must walk and what they must do."*[182] And through Moses, God told the people, *"You shall follow my rules and keep my statutes and walk in them."*[183]

---

[175] Matthew 4:23.
[176] Luke 17:11.
[177] John 4:1-42.
[178] Matthew 20:18.
[179] Genesis 5:24, RSV.
[180] Genesis 3:10-12.
[181] Genesis 6:9.
[182] Exodus 18:20, RSV.
[183] Leviticus 18:4, ESV.

Moses told the children of Israel in the wilderness, *"The LORD your God walks in the midst of your camp,"*[184] which means, your God is available to be "walked with," if you are willing to walk the way He wants you to.

Remember that old "sight gag" where somebody who has a very odd way of walking shows up to lead somebody to some destination and says, "Walk this way," and the person being led mimics the funny way of walking as they go on their way? Well, the world thinks that God's "way of walking" is a very funny way of walking these days—they love to laugh at it.

But the laugh may be on them when it turns out that God's "funny way" is the only way to walk with Him—and you can't get where you want to go if you don't walk with God to get there.

৵৽

So what does all this have to do with the Prophet Micah? In order to prophesy, Micah had to take a walk—literally. Unlike Isaiah, who lived in Jerusalem and knew the city like the back of his hand,[185] Micah was from a little town miles away.[186] And since you couldn't just email your message in like some "letter to the editor," Micah had to make the long journey to Jerusalem on foot to make the word of God known to the big-wigs in the big city.

Micah had to get "inside the beltway," as we might say today, because what he had to say was for the ears of the important people who were using their power to mess things up for the little people, in little towns like his, all over the country. And after he had walked the many miles to get to Jerusalem, Micah had to walk around the unfamiliar city trying to figure out where he could find the particular people God wanted him to deliver his prophecy to.

And what was his message?

---

[184] Deuteronomy 23:14, ESV.
[185] Isaiah 7:3.
[186] Micah 1:1.

"You're not walking the way God told you to. God said, 'Walk this way,' and you're not! And it's no laughing matter!"

❧❦

Some say the last verse in the Old Testament reading today is the most famous and significant verse in all of the prophets. Everybody says it's one of the most concise summaries of what biblical morality means: *"...do justice...love kindness and...walk humbly with your God."* I'm going to unpack each of these in a moment, but I want you to get the context first.

This is the prophet's answer to a question posed by the people listening to him: *"With what shall I come before the LORD?"*

In other words, "What can I do to get on God's good side?"

And then they offer some of their own ideas. But they only do so in response to an accusation from God that what they have been doing hasn't been right. Micah, Chapter 6, begins with the prophet announcing that God is taking them to court, the Court of Creation: *"Plead your case before the mountains and...hills...,"* Micah tells them.

❧❦

But before they get a chance to say anything, God presents His case against them:

> *"Hear, you mountains,*
> *the indictment of the LORD....*
> *The LORD has an indictment*
> *against his people..."*

And then Gods speaks directly to them:

> *"...what have I done to you?*
> *How have I wearied you?"*

God demands to know.

There is an old song that goes:

> "Why don't you love me like you used to do?
> How come you treat me like a worn-out shoe?

216

My hair's still curly and my eyes are still blue.
Why don't you love me like you used to do?"[187]

Though I doubt God has curly hair or blue eyes, the question in the song captures the spirit of God's complaint perfectly. The people who are supposed to be God's people—whose heritage includes the Exodus from Egypt and entry into the Promised Land in the face of fierce opposition that only God's power and grace could overcome—these people aren't acting like God matters to them anymore. They are not "walking" the way He told them to.

And to make matters worse, when God points out the obvious, and holds them accountable for not loving Him "the way they used to do," they act like they don't even know what He's talking about. It's like, now that God has taken them to court, all they can think to do is "plea-bargain": "Well, God, what will it take to calm You down and settle this little misunderstanding? Will the normal stuff be enough—or do you want us to do something excessive—or will it take something insanely extreme? We can kill a cow—or our whole herd—or our firstborn sons. What's Your pleasure, God?"

And here's where the prophet jumps back in—and good thing. I don't think they would have liked—or perhaps even lived through—God's response. But Micah pointedly reminds them that they already know the answer to their question. They know what God wants from them—just like their parents knew before them, and all their ancestors, all the way back to Moses bringing God's law down to them from Mount Sinai.

"He has told you, O man, what is good." Period! And God's definition of "good" does not change, no matter how much or how often ours does. Micah puts it in the form of a question, but everybody already knows the answer: *"What does the LORD require of you?"* Not "wish" you would do—not just "want" you to do—what does God *"require"* you to do?

---

[187] Hank Williams, "Why Don't You Love Me," 1950.

Here it is: Do justice. Love kindness. Walk humbly with your God.

That's it.

Now let's unpack it.

৯৯৯

"Do justice."

Do it. Not favor it. Not support it. Not desire it. *Do* it.

To the extent that you can do justice, do it. Make your world "right," everywhere and every time you have the chance. Do what is right for everybody, not just what is beneficial for you—and even when it is not beneficial to you, if it's the right thing to do—do it. Act to bring everything you can into harmony with God's righteous will.

Do justice.

৯৯৯

"Love kindness."

This is actually a bad choice of words for what the Hebrew is saying. It's a lot more than "kindness." "Mercy" would be better, and some translations use that. But it's even more than that.

It's the special Hebrew word for "steadfast love and loyalty"—God's kind of love that will do anything for His people and will not let them go, no matter what. In the New Testament, they call it "ἀγάπη"—"agápe."

I guess they thought it would seem odd to say, "love love." But what Micah means by this word is that God demands that we be totally committed to Him and to each other as covenant brothers and sisters. Maintain and show sincere, selfless, God-like love and loyalty to one another as we all show it to God.

৯৯৯

"Walk humbly with your God."

…which is what Micah did as he made his way up the long, hard road from his home to Jerusalem to demand that the people of Jerusalem do the same.

Micah would not have taken the physical walk if he had not first taken the spiritual and moral walk.

"Walk—humbly—with your God."

"Walk this way"—God's way. Go with Him where He wants to take you. Go with Him in the way He wants you to go. Go with Him, knowing always that He knows the right way—the good way—the best way. Go, knowing always that *He* is God—not you.

Go humbly—but not in the hope that by walking humbly with God you will get salvation as your reward. *"Walk humbly with your God,"* knowing that the walk began with God's free gift of salvation that no amount of humility, love or justice on your part could justify.

ॐ☙

And as you *"walk humbly with your God,"* there is another song you might consider. It begins like this:

"I'll walk with God, from this day on.
His helping hand, I'll lean upon.
This is my prayer, my humble plea:
May the Lord be ever with me."

And it ends like this:

"And I'll never walk alone
While I walk with God."[188]

ॐ☙

I wonder what Micah thought as he walked back home from Jerusalem. Maybe he asked himself: "Did anyone listen? Will anyone do what is right who wasn't doing it before? Will anyone love God and others with God's kind of love who didn't before?

---

[188] Nicholas Brodzsky and Paul Francis Webster, "I'll Walk with God," 1954.

Will anyone walk with God and walk God's way who was walking alone and away from God before I walked into town?"

None of that mattered, of course, as far as Micah's walk with God was concerned.

But people did listen—and have continued to listen—because here he is again, 27 *hundred* years later, inviting us to do justice, love kindness, and "take a walk"—a humble walk—with our God.

Thank you, Micah. We're still getting the message.

෧෴෧

From the Book of Malachi

Malachi 3:1, 3, 4 and 10 ESV

[1] *"Behold, I send my messenger, and he will prepare the way before me. And the Lord whom you seek will suddenly come to his temple; and the messenger of the covenant in whom you delight, behold, he is coming," says the* LORD *of hosts.*

[3] *He will sit as a refiner and purifier of silver, and he will purify the sons of Levi and refine them like gold and silver, and they will bring offerings in righteousness to the* LORD. [4] *Then the offering of Judah and Jerusalem will be pleasing to the* LORD *as in the days of old and as in former years.*

[10] *"Bring the full tithe into the storehouse, that there may be food in my house. And thereby put me to the test," says the* LORD *of hosts, "if I will not open the windows of heaven for you and pour down for you a blessing until there is no more need."*

ॐॐ

2 Corinthians 9:6-15 ESV

⁶ *The point is this: whoever sows sparingly will also reap sparingly, and whoever sows bountifully will also reap bountifully. ⁷ Each one must give as he has decided in his heart, not reluctantly or under compulsion, for God loves a cheerful giver. ⁸ And God is able to make all grace abound to you, so that having all sufficiency in all things at all times, you may abound in every good work. ⁹ As it is written,*

> *"He has distributed freely,*
> *he has given to the poor;*
> *his righteousness endures forever."*

¹⁰ *He who supplies seed to the sower and bread for food will supply and multiply your seed for sowing and increase the harvest of your righteousness. ¹¹ You will be enriched in every way to be generous in every way, which through us will produce thanksgiving to God. ¹² For the ministry of this service is not only supplying the needs of the saints but is also overflowing in many thanksgivings to God. ¹³ By their approval of this service, they will glorify God because of your submission that comes from your confession of the gospel of Christ, and the generosity of your contribution for them and for all others, ¹⁴ while they long for you and pray for you, because of the surpassing grace of God upon you. ¹⁵ Thanks be to God for his inexpressible gift!*

❧⊸⟨

26.

Refined Gifts and Givers

Malachi 3:1, 3, 4 and 10; 2 Corinthians 9:6-15 ESV

Actions and attitudes. We tend to focus on actions—what we *do*. God, Who is not indifferent to actions, seems more often more interested in attitudes—*why* we do what we do. If our actions need work, which they almost always do, God is more inclined to work on adjusting our attitudes than altering the offending actions, knowing, as God would, that our actions generally reflect and respond to our attitudes.

God says, *"Bring the whole tithe"* into His storehouse: an action. But Malachi doesn't say that God is going to come and haul us and our checkbooks into church and hover over us until we make the amount large enough to suit Him, and thereby fix our inadequate action. No, God is going to come to us and refine and purify our attitude about stewardship so that what we think about it is in keeping with what *He* thinks about it, which will ensure that what we *do* about it is pleasing and acceptable in His sight.

Consider that image for a moment. Malachi says, *"the Lord you are seeking…and Whom you desire is coming*—and when He does, He will refine and purify people just like someone would refine silver or gold."

Yikes!

225

And yet, how much better, more valuable and more wonderful is the purified version than the un-purified—of anything—including us?

What is God going to refine?

Not our actions, but our attitudes.

What does it mean for God to purify or refine an attitude?

It's an analogy, which allows for a little imaginative analysis. To be refined is to be put under some pressure that will so alter our natures that the impurities that have been so closely and tightly connected to our true essence will be dislodged and lose their hold on us. The more quickly we "let go" of those things that are not and should not be a part of us, the sooner the refining process will conclude.

The goal of refining precious metals is to get to the pure state—to produce, for instance, pure gold. God's goal for refining His people is to produce attitudes that are as nearly "pure God" as possible. God's attitude is: "Nothing but the best for those I love." We saw that in Creation, and in His gift of His Son, Jesus Christ. The attitude God is seeking in us as He refines us is the same: "Nothing but *my* best for the God Who loves me and gave Himself for me."

God is refining and purifying so that selfishness is removed from the essential generosity of spirit with which we were created. God is refining out fear and distrust and cynicism so that faith and hope and love remain as the motivating elements in our nature. God will work on these attitudes—*our* attitudes—until, as Malachi says, we present right offerings to the Lord—offerings pleasing to the Lord. The point is not the amount, but the motive—the attitude that wants to do what God wants us to do for the very same reasons God wants us to do it.

Sometimes, we are refined and purified by pressure—hardship—the refiner's fire. And other times, we are refined in unexpectedly gentle ways. *"Test Me,"* God says, which really means: "Test your faith in Me. Suspend your uncertainties and your worldly (and, therefore, sinful) inclinations for a while and let Me show you how unfounded they are. Let Me win you over to a refined and holy attitude by divine generosity rather than hardship and adversity."

And yes, this turns what I was saying at the beginning about actions and attitudes on its head, but only temporarily. God says, "Act, not in accordance with your attitude, but in direct contradiction to it, for a while—long enough for you to see what attitude is the purest and best for you. Let My response to your obedient actions show you the attitude you should adopt permanently to direct all your future actions. Let Me promote the proper attitude in you by showing you how I respond to proper actions. Let Me show you overwhelming blessings as though all of the goodness of heaven were falling on you."

The cynic will say, "Why do I have to do what You want me to do before You will shower me with all Your blessings. Just shower me, already. Maybe my attitude will change."

Except that it won't, because God *has* been generous already. *"The steadfast love of the LORD never ceases; his mercies never come to an end."*[189] Even when your attitude is bad and your actions are worse, God is still good.

But this business of refining and purifying requires some form of engagement between God and the individual. This is an experiment in generosity. This is practical application of a divine truth. This is God's effort to get our hearts and minds where they need to be—not for God's sake, but for ours.

And so there must be some pressure—even if it is wonderfully positive—to move the mind and the heart of a man or woman in the right direction. We are the ones who will benefit from a refined and purified attitude, not God. *We* are why God bothers. God says, "Do what I have told you to do and see if it will not do wonders for you." And if it does—and you see it and realize it—will not

---

[189] Lamentations 3:22, RSV.

your attitude change—and all the subsequent actions that come from your purified perspective?

Paul picks up the same theme in 2nd Corinthians. Where Malachi was talking about fulfilling the old biblical requirements to support the religious structure—meeting the operating budget—Paul is writing his friends in Corinth about contributions they had volunteered to make to foreign missions and benevolence work. And he deals with their attitudes more than their actions.

"Each man should give what he has decided in his heart to give…" according to his attitude, *"not reluctantly or under compulsion…."* Here's the refining and purifying of the attitude of generosity, faith, hope and love, *"for God loves a cheerful giver…."*

Again, attitude: *how* you give—not actions: how *much* you give.

Paul acknowledges the practical benefit of their action: *"This service that you perform is…supplying the needs of God's people."* But like God in Malachi, Paul is actually more interested in the refining, purifying benefit to the attitude that will *motivate* the action: *"Because of [this]…you have proved yourselves…"* Your actions demonstrate your attitude.

And Paul points out that this refining of their attitudes will serve to further refine the attitudes of other people—the recipients of their gift: *"…men will praise God…for your generosity in sharing with them and with everyone else. And in their prayers for you their hearts will go out to you…your generosity will result in thanksgiving to God."*

And if there is uncertainty on the Corinthians' part as to whether they should adopt the refined Christian attitude Paul promotes, he picks up Malachi's assurance of positive reinforcement: Act on the basis of God's call for generosity with your resources and see what God will do.

Paul says, *"God is able to make all grace abound to you, so that in all things at all times, [you will have] all that you need… He…will…supply and increase your store of seed and will enlarge the harvest of your righteousness. You will be made rich in every way so that you can be generous on every occasion…."*

God refines both the giver and the gift—the attitude and the action that results from it.

Next week, we will celebrate our commitment to the ongoing ministries of our church. We will bring forward our pledges for the coming year in an act of sacrificial worship. But more important than the act is the attitude of generosity and faith each pledge will symbolize. Whatever we possess in the way of resources, we share the refinement of faith that God has worked in us.

God has been generous to us in pouring out His blessings abundantly upon us. And God has made us a generous people, from the day He brought our fellowship into existence even until this day. That attitude of gratitude and generosity, of confidence that He will enable us to be generous for Him like He has been to us, is one of God's greatest blessings in us. And He continues to refine it within us so that we may be pure in presenting our offerings to Him, offerings pleasing in His sight.

What we want to give God is His gift to us.

What we are able to give God is His gift to us as well.

Thanks be to God for these and all His gifts! Amen.

వ—ఀ

Malachi 3:10-12 ESV

> *¹⁰ Can I forget any longer*
> *the treasures of wickedness*
> *in the house of the wicked,*
> *and the scant measure that is accursed?*
> *¹¹ Shall I acquit the man with wicked scales*
> *and with a bag of deceitful weights?*
> *¹² Your rich men are full of violence;*
> *your inhabitants speak lies,*
> *and their tongue is deceitful in their mouth.*

৵৽৹

Mark 8:1-9 ESV

¹ In those days, when again a great crowd had gathered, and they had nothing to eat, [Jesus] called his disciples to him and said to them, ² "I have compassion on the crowd, because they have been with me now three days and have nothing to eat. ³ And if I send them away hungry to their homes, they will faint on the way. And some of them have come from far away." ⁴ And his disciples answered him, "How can one feed these people with bread here in this desolate place?" ⁵ And he asked them, "How many loaves do you have?" They said, "Seven." ⁶ And he directed the crowd to sit down on the ground. And he took the seven loaves, and having given thanks, he broke them and gave them to his disciples to set before the people; and they set them before the crowd. ⁷ And they had a few small fish. And having blessed them, he said that these also should be set before them. ⁸ And they ate and were satisfied. And they took up the broken pieces left over, seven baskets full. ⁹ And there were about four thousand people. And he sent them away.

৵৽৹

27.

Enough and More

Malachi 3:10-12; Mark 8:1-9 ESV

We come to this message from the "messenger" of God—for that is what the name "Malachi" actually means—having all but completed our annual stewardship emphasis. At the same time, we are just beginning our preparations for Thanksgiving.

Now Malachi usually gets marched out in September or October to put a little pressure on God's people to pump up the financial dimension of their faithfulness. And just the mention of the name "Malachi" can cause many of the "better informed" (biblically) to go deaf or get distracted, detecting a guilt trip coming in the guise of a sermon.

On the other hand, who doesn't like a lovely story about Jesus providing an unplanned picnic for a multitude of people who couldn't have come up with a "Happy Meal" among them? The only guilt trip Jesus gives out there in the Gospel of Mark goes to His whiney disciples who wonder how He's going to whip up enough free food to feed all the folks who came to His Bible conference out there in the countryside.

But suppose we put these two passages together and pull out some practical applications for today.

First of all, let's recall that, in both cases, the economy was a mess. Times were hard in both time periods. The Persians were taxing the one group and the Romans were taxing the other. That's why the people were holding back in Malachi and had nothing to hold back—or bring forward—in Mark.

There just didn't seem to be enough of what people needed to go around. If demand exceeds supply, you better protect your insufficient supply so you don't run out of what you know you're going to need. It seemed the only sensible thing to do, under the circumstances.

But that attitude, as prudent and sensible as it seemed, left one key factor out of the equation: God. In the words of Malachi, God extended an invitation. In the deeds of Jesus, God delivered a demonstration. In both circumstances, the audience experienced a remarkable revelation.

৯৽৶

The best efforts and intentions of a sinful humanity—left to its own devices—will always fall short in its attempt to meet the needs of people and the planet. Even the best people "blow it" because our "best" is never good enough, in and of itself. And our normal efforts—not to mention our worst—are worse. And then there are those who are bad people, by our standards—or worse.

The bottom line is that many people suffer for real—and when we see them, we are afraid we might suffer, too. The temptation is to keep what little we have carefully conserved for the rainy day we know will come—perhaps as early as tomorrow. The temptation is to cut ourselves off—morally and emotionally—from the many who need so much—from people we cannot imagine how we could help. We do not want to lose what we have that we know we need for ourselves. We do not want to suffer, either, by seeing the reality of their fear and pain and need.

So where does God come into the picture?

In Malachi, God does not address the need for greater benevolence on the part of His people. Certainly, the Bible is filled with commands and admonitions to take care of those in the society who have genuine need. But before that, God is concerned with the relationship of people with Him. That is the first and always-central relationship, and it informs and determines the economic—as well as the spiritual—dimension of our lives.

That's why Jesus would tell people, *"Where your treasure is, there will your heart be also."*[190] And *"You cannot serve two masters*; you cannot make material things the main thing in your life."*[191] And *"Seek first the kingdom of God and his righteousness...."*[192]

And here's an interesting thing about how God engages the people He's disappointed with in Malachi.

God doesn't say, "I'm God. Give Me what I want—or else!" God can have what He wants—anything and everything He wants. "The Lord giveth and the Lord taketh away."[193] Right?

But God doesn't seem to want your "stuff"—even when He says, "Cough up a full 10 percent of what you have and drop it off at My place." That's not really the point.

ॐ•֍

God is challenging people who ought to know Him better than they do, to *get* to know Him better—by putting their money—their material possessions—their materialistic perspective—where God's mouth is, so to speak. God is saying to fearful people, "You don't really understand how the world works because you don't really understand how *I* work—am working—in this world of yours—the world I created and control—for your benefit."

It's funny how those who don't take God (whether the reality or the idea) seriously are always accusing those who do believe in

---

[190] Matthew 6:21, ESV.
[191] Matthew 6:24.
[192] Matthew 6:33, ESV.
[193] Job 1:21.

God and do take Him seriously, of not being "realistic." But who is the more realistic if reality really is what God says it is. God says that those who act in faith to enter into the supernatural relationship God offers them—in the way He requires—will have a relationship with Him that will make all of His grace and generosity available to them—to meet all the needs they know about. And then He will supply infinitely more grace and generosity than they could ever imagine—for meeting needs that never even crossed their minds—until they realized those needs were met, too.

When Christopher Columbus came back from the New World and told people what he found, many thought he was crazy—or, at least, "not realistic." The truth was that there was a reality they did not know and would not believe—real as it was and had always been. And Columbus would not "un-believe" what he had experienced just to be considered "realistic" by those who had not gone where he had.

If you will believe in God's promise and practice of grace and generosity to you by responding in kind—in faith—you will discover that you have been brought into God's new and wonderful "world," where the ways of this fallen, material world are surpassed and redeemed beyond imagining.

Whatever the material measure, the "reality" will be greater and richer and more joyous—as though (or because) the "windows of heaven" will be thrown open to you, and showers of blessings— God's most gracious of blessings—will be poured out upon you in your relationship with Him.

⤞⤝

Jesus didn't feed multitudes miraculously just because they were hungry—though He certainly had compassion on them for the material things they lacked. But notice that every time Jesus fed a crowd, He produced food they were not aware He had—food they were not aware *they* could have. Every time He fed people, there was enough for all of them to have all they wanted. And every time Jesus fed thousands with what seemed like nothing—from the world's realistic, materialistic perspective—and after everybody had enough, there was always much, much more left over.

Jesus was opening the windows of heaven and showing people the miraculous reality that awaits those who will believe and respond to God's out-of-this-world, yet for-this-world, reality of grace and generosity. You can be gracious because your God is gracious in His relationship with you. You can be generous with what you have because He is infinitely more generous with what He wants to—and will—give to you when you open your heart and your life and your self to let Him and His generosity in.

So here we are, considering how we will meet the ministry needs of this church in the year ahead, and at the same time, considering how we will give proper thanks for all the blessings that have been ours in this year now drawing to a close. Is it realistic to think—to believe—that these two activities are both, in some spiritual sense, part of a deeper, divine reality?

It depends, I guess, on what you bring to God in response to His challenge, or whether you have ever had this amazing Man feed you, enough and more, when you thought, realistically, there was nothing to be had.

Experience God's grace and generosity—enough and more.

འ–ཚ

Indices

Title	Page

A Chosen Servant 97
Abiding in God's Abiding Word 51

But If Not 165

Enough and More 231

For the Century Beyond 43

Happy Ending to a Sinful Story 31

In a Not-So-Perfect World 13
In the Presence of the Lord 83
It's Who You Know..185

Let's Take a Walk 213
Lost and Found..105

On Earth as It Is in Heaven......................................69
One Way or the Other..123

Put the Right Stuff In..155

Refined Gifts and Givers..225
Religion, Inside and Out..193
Remembering This and That 131
Restore Our Fortunes 59

Sheep and Their Shepherd 7
Since Before You Were Born 113

Title	Page

That the Next Generation Might Know 39
The Everlasting God..89

When God Puts Your Life Back Together................................ 143
When the Leader is Gone..77
When You Give God Your Sin 23
When You Think You're Going Under 203
Wise Ways in Wicked Days.. 175

Sermon Texts in Biblical Order

Text	Title	Page

Psalms

23	Sheep and Their Shepherd	5
32:1-5	In a Not-So-Perfect World	13
32:1-5	When You Give God Your Sin	22
51:1-17	Happy Ending to a Sinful Story	29
78:1-7	That the Next Generation Might Know	38
78:1-7	For the Century Beyond	42
119:11, 105	Abiding in God's Abiding Word	51
126	Restore Our Fortunes	57

Isaiah

6:1-13	On Earth as It Is in Heaven	66
6:1-13	When the Leader is Gone	66
6:1-13	In the Presence of the Lord	66
40:27-29	The Everlasting God	88
42:1-9	A Chosen Servant	95
55:6-9	Lost and Found	104

Jeremiah

1:1-10	Since Before You Were Born	111
17:5-8	One Way or the Other	121

Lamentations

3:19-26	Remembering This and That	128

Ezekiel

37:1-14	When God Puts Your Life Back Together	141

Daniel

1:1-21	Put the Right Stuff In	152
3:1-30	But If Not	161
5:1-31	Wise Ways in Wicked Days	171

Hosea

5:15—6:6	It's Who You Know	183

Text	Title	Page

Amos
5: 4, 7, 10, 21-24   Religion, Inside and Out.............. 192

Jonah
1:1-16   When You Think You're Going Under 200

Micah
6:6-8   Let's Take a Walk 211

Malachi
3:1, 3, 4 and 10   Refined Gifts and Givers.............. 223
3:10-12   Enough and More........................ 230

Sermon Texts in Biblical Order

Text	Title	Page

Matthew
8:23-27   When You Think You're Going Under 202
15:10-20   Put the Right Stuff In......................................154
16:1-3   Wise Ways in Wicked Days...........................174
18:23-35   Let's Take a Walk 212
26:36-42   But If Not..164

Mark
8:1-9   Enough and More 230

Luke
19:1-10   When You Give God Your Sin.......................22

John
5:21-29   When God Puts Your Life Back Together.142
10:1-11   Sheep and Their Shepherd 6
15:16-19, 26-27   Since Before You Were Born 112
16:2-22, 33   Remembering This and That........................129

Romans
8:1-11   One Way or the Other....................................122

2 Corinthians
9:6-15   Refined Gifts and Givers...............................224

Philippians
3:7-11   It's Who You Know.......................................184

Revelation
4:1-11   On Earth as It Is in Heaven............................68

Sermons from the Psalms and Prophets in Other Volumes

Text	Title	Page (in Other Volumes)

In *O Come, Let God Adore Us*

Psalms

126   Restore Our Fortunes 73

Isaiah

9:2, 6-7   Unto Us a Son is Given 189

11:1-10   Your Part in the Process............................. 103

11:1-10   Christmas Almost Didn't Happen 109

52:7-10   Going a Different Way 241

60:1-3, 19-20   Journey's End................................... 249

63 and 64   Come Down, Lord! 13

Jeremiah

33:14-16   The Days Are Coming… 27

33:14-16   What Are You Waiting For?...........................31

Micah

5:2-5a   The One of Peace.......................... 127

Zephaniah

3:14-20   O Come, Let God Adore Us 81

3:14-20   God's Joy..85

Malachi

3 and 4   And Along Came John 51

In *Walking with Jesus*

Isaiah

43:1-7   Just Passing Through 93

Text	Title	Page (in Other Volumes)

In *God's Purpose for Your Faith*

Malachi
3:10-12 Enough and More 91

In *From Jerusalem to Jericho*

Isaiah
25:6-9 Are You Going to the Party?.......................105
53:1-3 Not the Christ They Wanted.........................35

In *Traits of the Shepherd*

Psalms
23 Sheep and Their Shepherd ....??
92 Bearing Fruits 129

Isaiah
40:9-11 Traits of the Shepherd 96

In *Making Peace with Your Father*

Jeremiah
17:5-8 One Way or the Other....................................65

Malachi
3:1, 3, 4, 10 Refined Gifts and Givers 209

Sermons from the Psalms and Prophets in Other Volumes

Text   Title   **Page (in Other Volumes)**

In *The Empty God*

Hosea
5:15—6:6   It's Who You Know 143

In *Not Exactly What They Expected*

Isaiah
52 and 53   Who *Is* This Guy? 107

Jeremiah
31:31-34   Let's Try This Again 49

Zechariah
9:9-10   Look Who's Here 25

Sermon Texts in Lectionary Order

Date	Text	Page

Cycle A

Baptism of the Lord   Isaiah 42:1-9 95

Epiphany 4   Micah 6:6-8..211

Lent 1   Psalm 32:1-5 .... 13, 22

Lent 4   Psalm 23...5
Lent 5   Ezekiel 37:1-14....................................141
    Romans 8:1-11 122

Palm/Passion Sunday   Matthew 26:36-42..................................164

Easter 4   John 10:1-11 6

Proper 5 [19]   Hosea 5:15—6:6 183

Proper 10 [15]   Psalm 119:105 51
    Romans 8:1-11 122

Proper 15 [20]   Matthew 15:10-20.................................154

Proper 19 [24]   Matthew 18:23-35.................................212

Proper 21 [26]   Psalm 78:1-7 .... 38, 42
Proper 22 [27]   Philippians 3:7-11 184
Proper 23 [28]   Psalm 23...5

Proper 27 [32]   Psalm 78:1-7 .... 38, 42
    Amos 5:4, 7, 10, 24-27 192

Thanksgiving   2 Corinthians 9:6-15.............................224

Sermon Texts in Lectionary Order

Date	Text	Page
Cycle B		
Advent 3	Psalm 126	57
Epiphany 5	Isaiah 40:27-29	88
Lent 5	Psalm 51:1-17	29
	Psalm 119:11	51
Pentecost	Ezekiel 37:1-14	141
	John 15:16-19, 26-27	112
	John 16:2-22, 33	129
Proper 8 [13]	Lamentations 3:19-26	128
Proper 11[16]	Psalm 23	5
Proper 13 [18]	Psalm 51:1-17	29
Proper 23 [28]	Amos 5:4, 7, 10, 244-27	192
Proper 25 [30]	Psalm 126	57
Thanksgiving	Psalm 126	57

Sermon Texts in Lectionary Order

Date	Text	Page

Cycle C

Advent 2   Malachi 3:1, 3, 4 and 10......................223

Epiphany 4 [4]   Jeremiah 1:1-10...................................111
Epiphany 5 [5]   Isaiah 6:1-8 (9-13)................................66
Epiphany 6 [6]   Jeremiah 17:5-8...................................121

Lent 3   Isaiah 55:6-9...104
Lent 4   Psalm 32:1-5.................................... 13, 22
Lent 5   Psalm 126...57
                    Philippians 3:7-11 184

Trinity Sunday   Isaiah 6:1-8 (9-13)................................66
                    John 16:2-22, 33..................................129

Proper 6 [11]   Psalm 32:1-5.................................... 13, 22

Proper 16 [21]   Jeremiah 1:1-10...................................111

Proper 19 [24]   Psalm 51:1-17.......................................29

Proper 22 [27]   Lamentations 3:19-26 128

Proper 26 [31]   Psalm 32:1-5.................................... 13, 22
                    Luke 19:1-10...22

Sermon Texts in Lectionary Order

Date	Text	Page
Cycle ABC		
Presentation	Malachi 3:1, 3, 4 and 10	223
Ash Wednesday	Psalm 51:1-17	29
Holy Monday	Isaiah 42:1-9	95
Holy Saturday	Lamentations 3:19-26	128
Easter Vigil	Isaiah 55:6-9	104
	Ezekiel 37:1-14	141
Easter 4	Psalm 23	5
Holy Cross	Psalm 78:1-7	38, 42

Additional Scriptures Referenced

Text	Title	Page

Genesis

1:28	For the Century Beyond	45
2:7	When God Puts Your Life Back Together.	147
3	For the Century Beyond	45
3:8	Let's Take a Walk	213
3:10-12	Let's Take a Walk	214
5:24	Let's Take a Walk	214
6:9	Let's Take a Walk	214
12: 4-6	Let's Take a Walk	213
28:16	On Earth as It Is in Heaven	70
37:28	Let's Take a Walk	213

Exodus

1:8	Wise Ways in Wicked Days	177
3:10	Since Before You Were Born	117
3:11	Since Before You Were Born	118
14:21-31	Let's Take a Walk	213
18:20	Let's Take a Walk	214
34:5-7	For the Century Beyond	47

Leviticus

18:4	Let's Take a Walk	214

Numbers

32:13	Let's Take a Walk	213

Deuteronomy

12:5	On Earth as It Is in Heaven	71
23:14	Let's Take a Walk	215
29:29	A Chosen Servant	100
29:29	It's Who You Know	188

Joshua

11:1	Let's Take a Walk	213

Additional Scriptures Referenced

Text	Title	Page

Judges
21:25   Abiding in God's Abiding Word 54

1 Samuel
16:1-6   Since Before You Were Born 117

Job
1:21   Enough and More........................... 233
28:12, 23-24 When You Give God Your Sin......................26
31:15   Since Before You Were Born 114

Psalms
8:4-6   For the Century Beyond 44
37:17   Lost and Found............................ 102
39:4   It's Who You Know...................................... 187
46:10   *Preface* ix
51:3   In a Not-So-Perfect World............................20
90:2   For the Century Beyond 45
121:1-2   When the Leader is Gone...............................79
137:1-4   When God Puts Your Life Back Together 144
139:13   Since Before You Were Born...................... 114
139:13   It's Who You Know...................................... 187
139:14   Since Before You Were Born...................... 115

Proverbs
14:12   One Way or the Other.................................. 126
16:25   One Way or the Other.................................. 126

Isaiah
6:5   Since Before You Were Born...................... 118
7:3   Let's Take a Walk............................ 215
42:1-4   A Chosen Servant.................................99
44:2   Since Before You Were Born...................... 114
49:1, 5   A Chosen Servant.................................99
49:1-6   A Chosen Servant.................................99
50:4-11   A Chosen Servant.................................99

Additional Scriptures Referenced

Text	Title	Page

Isaiah (Continued)

50:6 — A Chosen Servant ... 99
52:13 — A Chosen Servant ... 100
52:13—53:12 — A Chosen Servant ... 99
53:3 — A Chosen Servant ... 99
53:4-5 — A Chosen Servant ... 100
53:6 — Sheep and Their Shepherd ... 12
53:6 — Happy Ending to a Sinful Story ... 32
53:6, 12 — A Chosen Servant ... 100
53:10, 12 — A Chosen Servant ... 100
55:6 — It's Who You Know ... 188
55:6-7 — Happy Ending to a Sinful Story ... 36
55:7 — When the Leader is Gone ... 79

Jeremiah

1:5 — It's Who You Know ... 187
23:5 — A Chosen Servant ... 101
29:13-14 — In the Presence of the Lord ... 85

Lamentations

1:1-2 — Remembering This and That ... 131
1:18 — Remembering This and That ... 134
1:22 — Remembering This and That ... 134
2:18-19 — Remembering This and That ... 135
3:1, 3 — Remembering This and That ... 135
3:22 — Refined Gifts and Givers ... 227

Ezekiel

37:1-14 — When God Puts Your Life Back Together ... 149

Daniel

1 — Wise Ways in Wicked Days ... 177

Hosea

2:19-20 — It's Who You Know ... 187
4:1, 6 — It's Who You Know ... 186

Additional Scriptures Referenced

Text	Title	Page

Amos
4:4-5   It's Who You Know 189
5:21   It's Who You Know 189

Micah
1:1   Let's Take a Walk 215

Habakkuk
2:14   On Earth as It Is in Heaven 74

Text	Title	Page

Matthew

3:17	A Chosen Servant	101
4:8-9	But If Not	169
4:10	But If Not	169
4:17	On Earth as It Is in Heaven	70
4:18, 21	When You Think You're Going Under	205
4:19	For the Century Beyond	45
4:23	Let's Take a Walk	214
6:9	On Earth as It Is in Heaven	70
6:10	When the Leader is Gone	75
6:12	In a Not-So-Perfect World	16
6:14-15	In a Not-So-Perfect World	16
6:21	Enough and More	233
6:24	Enough and More	233
6:33	Religion, Inside and Out	198
6:33	Enough and More	233
8:25	When You Think You're Going Under	205
10:29-31	It's Who You Know	187
13:34	That the Next Generation Might Know	40
18:3	On Earth as It Is in Heaven	72
18:22	In a Not-So-Perfect World	18
19:26	In a Not-So-Perfect World	19
20:18	Let's Take a Walk	214
22:37-39	Religion, Inside and Out	196
25:1-12	That the Next Generation Might Know	40
25:21	A Chosen Servant	102
25:40, 45	Happy Ending to a Sinful Story	34
28:19-20	Since Before You Were Born	117
28:20	Since Before You Were Born	119

Mark

3:13-14	Since Before You Were Born	117
4:38	When You Think You're Going Under	205
5:1-17	When You Give God Your Sin	24
13:11	Since Before You Were Born	119

Text	Title	Page

Luke

8:24	When You Think You're Going Under	205
10:1	Since Before You Were Born	117
11:29-30	When You Think You're Going Under	204
12:10	In a Not-So-Perfect World	16
15:3-7	Sheep and Their Shepherd	12
15:11-32	That the Next Generation Might Know	40
17:11	Let's Take a Walk	214
18:1-5	That the Next Generation Might Know	40
23:38-43	Wise ways for Wicked Days	180

John

1:14	Sheep and Their Shepherd	10
1:18	Sheep and Their Shepherd	10
3:16	In the Presence of the Lord	87
4:1-42	Let's Take a Walk	214
4:10	Sheep and Their Shepherd	10
8:31-32	Abiding in God's Abiding Word	56
14:3	On Earth as It Is in Heaven	73
14:18	When the Leader is Gone	78
19:10-11	But If Not	168

Acts

1:8	Since Before You Were Born	119
2:17-18	A Chosen Servant	102
8:26-38	A Chosen Servant	100

Romans

3:10	Happy Ending to a Sinful Story	32
3:23	Happy Ending to a Sinful Story	32
5:8	In a Not-So-Perfect World	16
5:8	Happy Ending to a Sinful Story	36
6:23	Happy Ending to a Sinful Story	37
8:19-22	When the Leader is Gone	74
8:29	A Chosen Servant	103

Text	Title	Page

Romans   (Continued)
8:38-39   It's Who You Know 189
12:1   A Chosen Servant 102

1 Corinthians
15:42-54   On Earth as It Is in Heaven 73
15:49   A Chosen Servant 102

2 Corinthians
3:12   A Chosen Servant 102
5:18-19   A Chosen Servant 101
5:20   For the Century Beyond 45
5:20   A Chosen Servant 102

Ephesians
1:7   In a Not-So-Perfect World 19
1:20   On Earth as It Is in Heaven 71

Philippians
2:6-7   On Earth as It Is in Heaven 70
2:7   It's Who You Know 188
2:8   A Chosen Servant 102
2:11   On Earth as It Is in Heaven 74

Colossians
1:19   On Earth as It Is in Heaven 71
1:19   A Chosen Servant 101
1:20   A Chosen Servant 101

1 Thessalonians
4:16-17   On Earth as It Is in Heaven 73

2 Timothy
2:8   A Chosen Servant 103
4:1   A Chosen Servant 103

Additional Scriptures Referenced

Text	Title	Page
Hebrews		
1:3	On Earth as It Is in Heaven	71
10:12	A Chosen Servant	103
James		
1:5-6	Since Before You Were Born	118
1:5-6	It's Who You Know	188
1:17	When You Give God Your Sin	24
1 John		
1:5	When You Give God Your Sin	24
1:8	Happy Ending to a Sinful Story	32
1:9	When You Give God Your Sin	27
1:9	Happy Ending to a Sinful Story	37
3:20	When You Give God Your Sin	26
1 Peter		
1:20	A Chosen Servant	101
1:25	Abiding in God's Abiding Word	54
Revelation		
1:17-18	On Earth as It Is in Heaven	71

www.ingramcontent.com/pod-product-compliance
Lightning Source LLC
Chambersburg PA
CBHW020848090426
42736CB00008B/289